# THIS **WAR** SO
# HORRIBLE

HIRAM SMITH WILLIAMS.
From an 1862 steel engraving that appeared in *The Coachmakers Magazine*.
By Jeanette Boughner

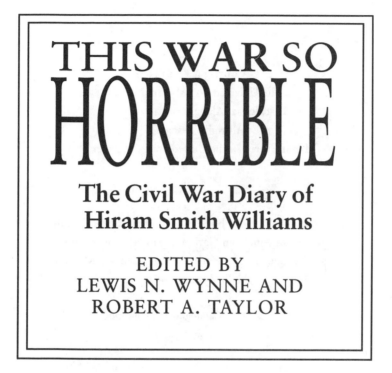

# THIS WAR SO
# HORRIBLE

The Civil War Diary of
Hiram Smith Williams

EDITED BY
LEWIS N. WYNNE AND
ROBERT A. TAYLOR

The University of Alabama Press
Tuscaloosa & London

∞

The paper on which this book is printed meets the minimum
requirements of American National Standard for Information
Science-Permanence of Paper for Printed Library Materials,
ANSI Z39.48-1984.

Library of Congress Cataloging-in-Publication Data

Williams, Hiram Smith, 1833–1921.
    This war so horrible : the Civil War diary of Hiram Smith Williams
/   edited by Lewis N. Wynne and Robert A. Taylor.
    p.  cm.
    Includes bibliographical references and index.
    ISBN 0-8173-0642-0
    1. Atlanta Campaign, 1864.  2. Williams, Hiram Smith, 1833–1921—
Diaries.  3. Confederate States of America.  Army.  Corps of
Engineers.  4. Soldiers—Alabama—Diaries.  5. United States—
History—Civil War, 1861–1865—Personal narratives, Confederate.
I. Wynne, Lewis Nicholas.  II. Taylor, Robert A., 1958–  .
III. Title.
E476.7.W55  1993
973.7'378—dc20                                        92-25867

British Library Cataloguing-in-Publication Data available

For Debra, Patrick, and Lisa Wynne
                                    Lewis N. Wynne
To the memory of Anna P. Hagymasi
                                    Robert A. Taylor

# Contents

# Maps

# Preface

The American Civil War has fascinated professional historians and the general public throughout the thirteen decades that have passed since the end of that great conflict. Hollywood probably has dedicated as many feet of film to this single topic as to any other, and authors have used the war as a vehicle for presenting a variety of plots, good and bad. Almost always, the war has been portrayed as a grand sweep of clashing armies, of heroic men and women, and of titanic struggles between competing moral issues. One idea has remained constant in all of these portrayals, and that is the idea that, above all else, the Civil War was a romantic epic in our history.

The persistence of the romantic myths of the Civil War, despite the widespread destruction of human life and real property, is evident in the state flags, state seals, football helmets, and marching bands that constitute a part of our daily lives. Of course, the ubiquitous pickup trucks, driven by thousands of urban and rural "rednecks," North and South, with their messages of "Forget Hell!" or "If your heart ain't in Dixie, get your ass out!" serve to remind us that the romantic myths of the War Between the States are stronger today than perhaps they were 130 years ago. Almost from birth, Americans are forced to take sides in this long-finished conflict. Even professional historians get caught up in the romantic depictions of this war, and few can escape a vicarious identification with the individuals involved. The result is a multitude of books about officers and leaders, who are described with such adjectives as bold, dashing, daring, or gallant and who are identified as a cavalier, dragoon, knight, or chevalier.

There was another Civil War, however. A war that was not a series of epic clashes between titans or a romantic tournament with gaily clad knights. It was instead a simple quest for survival. So the Civil War was to Hiram Smith Williams.

What follows is an "eye level" history of the Atlanta Campaign and its aftermath, not from the perspective of some heroic "man on horseback," but from the observations of Hiram Smith Williams, a private in the 40th Alabama Volunteer Infantry Regiment. The great movements and critical engagements of Federal and Confederate armies, so greatly admired by military professionals, academics, and armchair strategists, are reduced to nothing more than endless days and nights of marching, brief and bloody episodes of mayhem, months of privation and hardships, moments of gut-wrenching fear, and the sudden unexpectedness of death.

The lives of common soldiers provide valuable insights into the realities of the face of battle. In 1943, Bell Irvin Wiley wrote his seminal *Life of Johnny Reb,* which focused attention on the daily concerns of the enlisted soldiers in the Confederate army. *Johnny Reb* was a groundbreaking attempt to cut through the hero worship of the past and to provide a look at the realities of the war for the mass of Southern soldiers. Although Wiley's work did not end the "cult of the hero," it did expose the public to an important facet of the tragedy of war. Interest in the common soldier in all wars was further heightened during the 1940s when the world became intimately acquainted with Willie and Joe, William Mauldin's hapless heroes of World War II. Hiram Smith Williams would have thoroughly enjoyed the mishaps and misadventures of Willie and Joe. Even more recent historians, such as Reid Mitchell, Gerald F. Linderman, and James I. Robertson, have recognized the value of examining the activities and thoughts of common soldiers, and slowly a body of documentation is being compiled that will provide much more useful insights into these questions. In virtually every way, Hiram Smith Williams conforms to the composite picture of the average soldiers drawn in the writings of these historians. He, like his fellow soldiers in the Confederate and Union armies, displayed an almost morbid fascination with death, wrestled constantly with the horrors of mass slaughter, worried about friends and family left behind, and complained mightily about the regimentation of army life.

Hiram Smith Williams was an unusual Confederate, and the fact that he was a native of New Jersey, a relatively recent arrival in the South (1859), and a member of the middle class without ties to the slaveholding aristocracy certainly subjected him to additional stress. Why he chose to enlist in the Confederate Army can only be a matter of speculation. Although he spent his early adulthood traveling across the Midwest as a proponent of the American Know-Nothing party, his xenophobia, which was shared by many other Northerners, does not seem a sufficient answer to the question. Neither his late arrival in the South nor his status as a carriage maker seems adequate explanation for his willingness to risk life and limb for Southern nationalism. Thus, it is possible only to speculate about his reasons for casting his lot with the South.

Three major reasons for his decision to join the military come readily to mind. First, Hiram Smith Williams was a social creature, who always enjoyed the company of others. Throughout his diaries, including the twelve unpublished diaries of the 1850s, social activities figure prominently in his thoughts. To such an individual, the possibility of not joining friends and neighbors in what initially promised to be an exciting adventure would have been unthinkable. Perhaps caught up in the excitement of war preparations and infected with the enthusiasm of his peers, Williams simply joined the army on the spur of the moment. If that is true, and there is no real way to determine this fact, he would not have been alone in doing so.

A second reason might have been that the possibility of remaining in Alabama, particularly in the city of Mobile, was enough to persuade him that service in the military might not be such a bad experience. The 40th Alabama was formed in Mobile, and the unit initially participated in the defense of the city. Williams' skills as a mechanic and carpenter allowed him quickly to find an alternative to the endless marching and drilling of an infantry private. The Confederate Navy, desperate to improve the number and quality of its ships, actively sought the services of such men. Along with hundreds of civilians who worked in the shipyards, Williams and other similarly skilled army troops worked to satisfy the demand for ships. After he was detached from his unit, Williams' life in Mobile was little different from that of civilians. His wages, set by the Confederate Congress at $3.00 per day or $2.40 and rations as compared to the $11.00 a month paid to soldiers on duty in the field, provided him with enough money to live well in wartime Mobile. He quickly became active in the local theater, participated in various social activities, and apparently became involved in fraternal organizations, such as the Masons. The likelihood that an able-bodied man in wartime Mobile, seeking social acceptance by society and not in uniform, would find success was small. Thus military service might have provided Williams with the reason and the means to stay in the city.

A third potential reason for Williams' decision to join the army is that he might have wished to avoid the draft. Since the exact date of his enlistment is not known, it is possible that he enlisted in 1862 in order to ensure that he would be assigned to a company that included friends from Livingston, Alabama, the rural village he called home. Inasmuch as the Confederate Congress enacted the first draft law in April 1862, perhaps Williams felt he had to volunteer in order to have some voice in his unit assignment. This possibility coincides with the organization of the 40th Alabama Volunteer Infantry Regiment in May 1862.

For whatever his reasons, in 1862 Hiram Smith Williams enlisted in the army and, when his unit was sent to join Confederate forces in Mississippi, he stayed behind. When he was called into active service for the Atlanta campaign, he tried to find a way to stay in Mobile, even to the point of transferring from army service to the navy. When his efforts failed, he obeyed his orders and joined his company in Georgia.

Always looking for ways to improve his condition in life, he once again utilized his skills as a craftsman to secure detached duty away from the frontlines. In doing so, he served as a member of General Alexander P. Stewart's Pioneer Corps. As a member of this specialized group, Williams and his fellow soldiers assumed responsibility for building fortifications, cutting roads, constructing bridges and hospitals, and completing other general engineering tasks assigned by the corps commander. In most instances, this unit operated behind the lines of battle, but occasionally it was caught in the crossfire of competing armies. When these instances occurred, Williams demonstrated a cool head and brave heart. Certainly no coward, he nevertheless demonstrated a desire to ensure his personal safety as much as possible. Very little has been written about the Pioneer Corps, and, if for no other reason, Williams' descriptions of the activities of this specialized group of soldiers make this diary an important contribution to the literature on the war.

As a skilled journalist who had published in newspapers and magazines, Williams used his literary skills to capture the harshness and humor of a soldier's life. His diary is unusual because very little in the way of textual editing was needed. Indeed, the only changes made were to convert shorthand symbols, like ampersands and abbreviations, into full words and to correct his phonetic spellings of place names. His notations on movements and battles are frequently more detailed and illuminating than those of the commanders of the units involved.

For some historians, the richness of detail in Hiram Smith Williams' diary would be a temptation to branch out into larger discussions about the daily life of soldiers, their worries, and their opinions. We have deliberately limited such discussions to a minimum. We believe that such discussions, while important, would detract from the essential qualities of his diary. For the same reason, we have avoided prolonged examinations of the Atlanta campaign and the 40th Alabama. The locale is unimportant and could have been any campaign in the war. So, too, are the various battles. Williams was not involved in most of the combat experiences of the 40th Alabama, and his experiences were not the experiences of the survivors of that unit. What is most important about this journal is that it is one of the most articulate and descriptive narratives of the individual soldier's efforts to survive in a world apparently gone mad. It should be respected for that alone.

Hiram Smith Williams wrote for posterity. Aware that his diary would be read by others, he took care with how he composed his notes. Several persons who have read the diary in both its original form and in transcription have remarked on how well it is written. The absence of crossed-out words, erasures, or incomplete thoughts gives the impression of postwar editing. Persistent inquiries to members of the Williams family produce the same answer. Hiram Smith Williams wrote in the field, and, once the war was over, put his diary away and never worked on it again. An examination of twelve additional diaries from the decade of the 1850s shows them to be similarly well written. Certainly any postwar editing would have given him the opportunity to "punch up" his war experiences and to make himself appear more heroic. He did not do this kind of postwar editing.

Apparently Williams applied the same meticulous attention to his writing that he gave to manufacturing carriages and wagons. Proud of his abilities as a wordsmith, he obviously thought carefully, organized cogently, chose words meticulously, and then brought thoughts, organization, and words together in a decisive and forceful way. An exceedingly proud man, according to his granddaughter, he was keenly aware that future generations might read his writings, and he obviously wanted to leave behind a record that reflected his pride in his literary skills.

Several people have contributed to making this work a reality. Hiram Smith Williams' granddaughter, Margaret Williams Rainwater, and her husband, Robert, share his sense of history and have preserved many of his writings. Their sense of family history is remarkable and deserving of praise.

David S. Neel of Birmingham, Alabama, provided a photocopy of Judge Samuel Sprott's writings on the 40th Alabama. David was also helpful with suggestions about other sources. Professor John M. Belohlavek of the University of South Florida also provided a source of criticism and helpful commentary. Debra Teicher helped with the proofing; Marilyn Potts, our secretary, assumed a greater workload so that we could devote our time to transcribing the fading diary; and Carolyn J. Barnes, a graduate assistant at the University of South Florida, helped by listening to us and by offering suggestions for missing or faded words. Thank you.

Jeanette Boughner, a gifted Tampa artist, provided the drawings for this work. Her ability to work from faded photographs, fuzzy photocopies, and complex military maps lends clarity and understanding to the complexities of the mind of Hiram Smith Williams and the movements of great armies in conflict.

The author of this diary, Hiram Smith Williams, deserves all the credit. The mistakes, if any, are ours.

LEWIS N. WYNNE
ROBERT A. TAYLOR

# THIS **WAR** SO
# HORRIBLE

# Introduction

Hiram Smith Williams was born on July 27, 1833, at West Bloomfield (now Montclair), New Jersey, the third child of John and Martha Hopping Carter Williams. The Williams family was prominent in New Jersey social and business circles and traced their presence in North America to the early 1600s. The family claimed a direct relationship with Oliver Cromwell, and their immigration to the North American colonies may have been the result of the Restoration of the English monarchy in 1660.

Throughout the colonial period, the Williams family prospered, acquiring large tracts of land and numerous businesses. The family split over the question of American independence, and the victory by the Americans presented difficulties for the family. Hiram S. Williams' great-grandfather, Nathaniel, was a committed supporter of the Crown and was placed in jail in Morristown, New Jersey, by the local Committee of Safety. He died in 1782 from smallpox. His property was confiscated by American authorities at the end of the war, and his widow was forced to purchase it from the new authorities. As a result of the family's Revolutionary War experience, part of the family voluntarily exiled itself to Nova Scotia, but part remained in New Jersey.

By the 1830s, the Williamses were solidly entrenched and socially respectable members of the community surrounding West Bloomfield. Landowners and farmers, the Williams family also included a number of artisans and craftsmen, who worked as coopers and carriage makers. In addition, various members of the family served in a number of local political offices and appeared to enjoy the confidence of the community.[1]

Thus, the world to which Hiram Smith Williams was born in July 1833 was that of a comfortable and financially secure middle-class family. As a child, he attained a common school education and acquired an interest in prose writing and poetry. An 1862 sketch of his early life in *The New York Coachmakers Magazine* described an almost idyllic life as a student: "It was during this time that he manifested a taste for and a desire to use his pen, which resulted in the production of numerous pieces, in poetry and prose. Especially did he delight in poetry, and it was his habit to take a favorite piece found in his school-book, go out to the woods alone, and there read it aloud to the passing winds."[2] His love of writing continued throughout his life, and Williams frequently contributed pieces to a variety of magazines under the *nom de plume* of "Hebron Bell."

On June 10, 1850, Hiram Williams left West Bloomfield for Newark to become an apprentice in the carriage shop of Daniel DeCamp. Dissatisfied with the level of training he received from DeCamp, Williams left Newark in 1852 and entered into an apprenticeship with Wood and Tomlinson, a carriage firm in Bridgeport, Connecticut.[3]

Upon the completion of his apprenticeship in 1854, Hiram Williams left the certainty and security of mechanic's life on the East Coast to take up a career as a wandering journalist, contributing articles to various newspapers and magazines. For three years, he drifted from city to city in Ohio, contributing articles to various magazines and becoming involved in the promotion of the Know-Nothing party.

Original sketch by Hiram Smith Williams of himself talking with individuals in
Missouri during his 1856 campaign for Millard Fillmore (Rainwater Collection)

Original sketch by Hiram Smith Williams depicting a more leisurely aspect of his campaign efforts for Millard Fillmore in 1856 (Rainwater Collection)

The official charter for the American Nativist Party Council, issued May 27, 1856, to Hiram Smith Williams, J. H. Dwyer, and J. H. Wigginton of Madison, Ohio (Rainwater Collection)

In 1856, he served as the president of the Madison, Ohio, council of the American Order. As president of the local group, Williams led a movement seeking reinstatement in the National Council, which had expelled the Ohio group for failing to support the nomination of Millard Fillmore as the presidential candidate for the party in the election of 1856. Addressing a formal petition to the National Council on March 20, 1856, Williams and his fellow members pledged to support the principle that "Americans Shall Rule Americans" and promised "not to act, Either directly or indirectly, with any other political party or parties, So long as we remain in this Order."[4]

During the election campaign of 1856, Williams traveled throughout Ohio, Indiana, Illinois, and Iowa on behalf of the Know-Nothing party. He filed periodic reports with the Greenfield (Ohio) *Republican,* signing his columns "Patent Rights" and "Excubitor." As Williams visited the various towns along his route, he worked diligently to promote the cause of Fillmore and the Know-Nothings and spoke to several rallies. The Democrats were "truckler[s] to the South," he argued while Republicans were "tools in the hands of Northern Abolitionists." Only a Fillmore victory would assure "a triumphant vindication of American principles, to the utter rout of the foreign Democracy and truckling Republicans."[5]

The election of James Buchanan to the presidency in 1856 was disheartening to Williams. The failure of the Know-Nothing effort ended his interest in national politics for several years, and he brought his career as a political activist to a close. Even his commentaries to the press stopped, since, as he wrote in 1861, "politics changed too fast for my muse to keep up with the times, so I dropped it."[6]

In his diary, Williams evaluated the impact of the extreme partisanship that marked the 1856 election:

> If we could while midst the confusion
> We would arrive at this conclusion

We'll have 3 presidents the next four years
And our Union will be dissolved
In civil war we'll be involved[7]

By 1857, Hiram Williams had tired of Ohio and left for Illinois. Shortly thereafter, he moved to Council Bluffs, Iowa, and supported himself by "hunting and fishing." In 1858, he spent one year teaching school in St. Joseph, Missouri. Despite his professed dislike of Southern fire-eaters and despite his prediction of a possible civil war, in 1859, Williams left Missouri for Alabama and soon settled in the vicinity of Livingston, located in the heart of the state's plantation belt. Enamored with the bucolic atmosphere of this isolated village, he described it as "one of the most pleasant of the many delightful rural villages of Alabama."[8]

For a Northerner deep in the heart of Dixie, Williams must have adapted well to his new environment. What exactly his position was on the institution of slavery is hard to determine with certainty, although he made a cryptic reference to it in an 1856 diary. Reflecting on the emergence of the Republican party Williams noted that the Republicans "love a negro better than a man that's white."[9] His opinion of Southern Democrats was little more charitable, and the same year, he composed a verse of political doggerel in which he entreated, "Let the fire-eaters of the South stay there/Is my earnest, heart felt prayer."[10] Perhaps Williams' Know-Nothing principles led him to accept residency in a Democratic South as a more acceptable alternative to living in the North with its growing Abolitionist movement. His postwar allegiance to the Democratic party tends to support this idea.

While a resident of Livingston, Williams contributed articles to various magazines and maintained an ongoing correspondence with Ezra M. Stratton, the editor of *The New York Coachmakers Magazine.* Using the character, "Clarence Clifford," Williams contributed a number of articles to the magazine. These articles received such favorable responses that Stratton wrote to Williams in March 1861 requesting a brief biographical sketch and a photograph to appear in the 1862 volume of the magazine. "There appears to be an unusual desire to see the portrait of the author of Clarence Clifford in the magazine," he wrote, "And I have therefore to request that you would consent to my having it engraved for the 1[st] n[umber] of Vol[ume] 4."[11] A month earlier, Stratton had written to tell Williams of a fan letter that had been sent to the magazine and enquired about the identity of Clifford. "A girl 20 years old, an only daughter, single [and] the daughter of a wealthy farmer!" wrote Stratton, "Whew! Who would not [want to] be the author of Clifford?"[12]

Certainly the topic of a possible conflict between North and South was discussed in his communications with Stratton, since the editor made note of the troubled times and escalating tensions between North and South. "Times are awful [and] many ships shut-up. . . . I am afraid we must have [un]civil war!" wrote Stratton in February 1861. As late as March 5, 1861, he was hopeful that war could be avoided and asked Williams, "Can you add to my sub[scription] list in Ala[bama]? I wish for no secession in the Mag[azine and] do not intend to touch upon the subject in its columns."[13]

When the biographical sketch of Williams finally was published in the *Coachmakers Magazine* in May 1862, the question of secession and war had become moot. By April 1861, the nation was engulfed in the horror of civil war, and Hiram Smith Williams was just another of the millions of Americans who watched and hoped the conflict would end quickly.

Early predictions of a short war did not pan out, so faced with the prospect of being drafted into Confederate service, Hiram Smith Williams, sometimes calling himself Henry Smith Williams or H. Smith Williams, enlisted in the McCullough Avengers, which became Company C of the 40th Alabama Volunteer Infantry Regiment. Organized in May 1862 in Mobile, under the command of Colonel John H. Higley, the 40th Alabama had an active role in several major theaters of the war. From May until October 1862, the 40th Alabama served as part of the Army of Mobile, a force charged with keeping this vital port open to Confederate commerce. After a brief interlude at Columbus, Mississippi, the regiment was transferred to General John C. Pemberton's Vicksburg command.[14]

Hiram Smith Williams, however, did not serve actively with the 40th Alabama in the Mississippi theater. As a skilled craftsman, he was able to secure work as a naval carpenter on detached duty. In March 1863, several companies of the Fortieth participated in the struggle against General Frederick Steele's Bayou Campaign. On July 4, 1863, the 40th Alabama was among the Confederate units captured at Vicksburg and paroled. By September of that year, the regiment had been reconstituted and fought as part of the Army of Tennessee at Missionary Ridge in late November. Soon after, the Army of Tennessee, along with the 40th Alabama, went into winter quarters at Dalton, Georgia.[15]

Although the 40th Alabama played an active role in the war in Mississippi, Hiram S. Williams was not a participant. Immediately after his enlistment in Company C of the 40th, he was assigned to detached duty in Mobile. His skills as a carpenter and carriage maker were put to good use by the military authorities in the town, particularly the Confederate Navy. During this sojourn in the port city, Williams developed an active social life, spending much of his free time as an actor in the local theatrical productions. In addition to his career in the theater, he participated in a number of clubs and organizations. Attracted to the pomp and ritual of secret organizations, as evidenced by his prior association with the Know-Nothings, he joined the Order of Royal Arch Masons, Chapter 21, in Mobile. When he departed the city in February 1864, he carried with him a letter from the Order that designated him as a "member in good standing."[16]

Fascinated with the pomp and ceremony of secret societies, Hiram Smith Williams was a member of the Royal Arch Masons, headquartered in Mobile, Alabama. He maintained his ties with masonic orders throughout his life. (Rainwater Collection)

April 19, 1864 entry in Hiram Smith Williams' diary commenting on a review of the Army of Tennessee by General Joseph Eggleston Johnston

At the beginning of the Atlanta campaign in 1864, he applied for a transfer to the Confederate naval force in Mobile Bay. He must have been optimistic about his chances for staying in the city he loved because the Richmond government had published orders in the October 13, 1863, Mobile *Register and Advertiser* that men on detached service could not be transferred back to their units without the concurrence of both the naval and army commander. Although the naval commander, Admiral Franklin

Title page for Volume II of Hiram Smith Williams' diary. This volume deals with the Battle of Atlanta, the retreat from that city, and the final campaign in the Carolinas.

Buchanan, approved the request, Army commanders denied it, and Williams was ordered to report to his company, which was in winter quarters in Dalton, Georgia.[17] When his request for an interservice transfer was rejected, he packed his belongings and set out to rejoin his company.

His sense of loss of place was profound, for Williams had established a wide circle of friends in Mobile. Williams recorded this sense of loss in the opening lines of his diary for 1864 when he bade farewell to all "the pleasant places, the theatre, the social hoards [sic] . . . the friends I have found."[18]

On February 20, 1864, Williams reported to his regiment in Georgia. Toward the end of that month, he, along with others in his regiment, participated in the opening skirmishes of General William Tecumseh Sherman's campaign against General Joseph Eggleston Johnston and the Army of Tennessee. On March 10, however, he got the opportunity to leave his front-line company and to become a member of the Pioneer Corps, or engineers, attached to various divisional headquarters of the Army.[19]

Although somewhat reluctant to leave his comrades in Company C, Williams nevertheless eagerly accepted the assignment. Much like his 1862–63 assignment in Mobile, the Pioneer Corps spared him the rough life of a front-line soldier. While the element of danger was always present, Pioneers were seldom required to participate in direct assaults on enemy positions or to perform dangerous picket duty. In his diary entry for that day, he noted the advantages that being a Pioneer brought— better quarters and rations, for starters. Even more desirable, however, was the opportunity to leave the front lines and to avoid the routine that marks camp life for all armies. "Well, what have I made by the exchange?" he asked himself. The answer was very positive: "A good deal in my way of thinking. First, I have no drill. Secondly, roll call but once-a-day, in camp three times, with all one's accoutrements on. We stand guard here but once in about twenty days, in camp once in every three or four days. To be sure we have to work now and then, but I do not engage in any *battle* [emphasis his]."[20]

For Williams, the transfer to the Pioneer Corps was not a question of courage, for he frequently encountered danger while working on roads and fortifications. "I do not claim to be blessed with any extra amount of bravery," he wrote during the Battle of New Hope Church when his company could not work on breastworks because of intense enemy fire, "but at all events, I can safely say I did not exhibit quite as much cowardice as some in the company."[21] For a less than enthusiastic warrior, as Williams freely admitted he was, the Pioneer Corps offered a modicum of safety and the opportunity to be more of an observer than a soldier. Yet when duty demanded that he be a frontline soldier, he accepted this assignment without complaint.

As a member of the Pioneers, Williams frequently was called upon to build hospitals and to assist surgeons in the operating room. His descriptions of the horror of amputations, the agony of the wounded, and the loneliness of the dead and dying are graphic and thought provoking. As the war progressed, he questioned its validity more and more.[22] "War at best is horrible," he wrote at the beginning of the Atlanta campaign, "but this [one], so unholy, so bitter, in its progress . . . so absurd as to the establishment of any great and vital principle, is the worst record upon the pages of modern history."[23] By August 31, 1864, with the loss of Atlanta, his attitude had become stronger, and he concluded: "This horrid useless waste of human life, this wholesale butchery is terrible and should damn the authors through all time."[24] Throughout his diary, Williams constantly questioned the motives of the "military power" that ran the war, as well as those politicians he held responsible for starting and continuing the struggle.[25]

The war did provide Williams with moments of humor and nostalgia, and his descriptions of veterans playing cards while under attack by artillery, of the pleasures of a warm hut and dry bed, of the seeming ineptness of officers, and the stupidity of army rituals were typical of armies in every war. Even on the retreat from Atlanta, he found humor in the plight of a young woman and her beau surprised by a battalion of soldiers who had taken their pants off to ford a stream. Another time the plight of an officer scurrying to leave the area of an artillery barrage and losing his weapon and his teakettle provoked a humorous comment from Williams.[26]

Similarly, Williams experienced the loneliness and isolation from friends and family that the demands of war produced. Throughout his entries, he referred to the tragedy of soldiers dying in places far from home and kin, to the terrible ache that memories of home produced, and to the joys of being able to experience a comradeship akin to familial ties with his fellow soldiers. A letter from his brother, Edmund, brought news of friends and family in New Jersey and invoked strong emotions about home.[27]

Socially adept and keenly observant, Williams noted the people and geography of places he visited. While employed in cutting timber in Tilton, he observed, "There are plenty of girls in this part of Georgia, but very few goodlooking ones."[28] Still he found enough acceptable girls to fill his social calendar when time and circumstances permitted. A soldier "must have plenty of *impudence*," he noted, "if he expects to get along in society now." Soldiers without this critical component "had better remain in camp altogether and never pretend to pass an hour socially among the softer sex."[29]

The defeat of General John Bell Hood and the Army of Tennessee at Atlanta marked the beginning of the final stages of existence for the Confederacy. Williams applied for a transfer to his old company, and on November 6, 1864, was ordered to report to his regiment, which was again stationed at Mobile. He arrived in Mobile on November 20 and immediately visited his friends. Little is known of his activities in Mobile from November 1864 until he and his regiment were ordered to South Carolina on January 29, 1865. During this period, Williams made no entries in his diary, and the only record extant is a letter, dated January 22, 1865, from his company commander, Captain Thomas M. Brunson, to the Provost Marshal Captain William E. Yancey, requesting a pass for Williams to visit Mobile because "his effects are all in the City of Mobile and he is very anxious to fix up things Suitable to leave for a considerable length of time [due to] the uncertainty of our forces being able to hold the City."[30]

From Mobile to Bentonville, North Carolina, where he was captured on March 19, 1865, Williams soldiered with the 40th Alabama. At Bentonville, however, the fatigue of constant marching and the growing sense of futility at the continuance of the war took over. When his unit broke through the lines of the 14th Corps of the Army of the Cumberland and this advantage was not exploited by the Confederate command, he refused to continue to fight, "As I had no idea of going back, I lay down below our breastworks and was captured about an hour [later]."[31]

For Hiram Smith Williams, one phase of the war was over, but another was just beginning. With other prisoners of war, he was transported by ship to a prison camp at Point Lookout, Maryland. Although the bullets were no longer flying, the war was far from over for him, and he found life in the prison camp extremely hard. Point Lookout was among the worst of the Federal prisons, and officials forced 20,000 prisoners to live in temporary shelters year round. Food and clothing were in short supply and could be had in sufficient amounts only through a complex system of purchase and bribery.[32]

Allowed to receive mail and money from relatives in New Jersey, he was frustrated by the failure of his family to take advantage of the privilege. On April 26, he voiced his frustrations in his dairy. "For a week past," he wrote, "I have been looking for and expecting money from my brother, but not a line have I had, nor a dollar. Why it is I cannot imagine." Alone in a hostile prison environment that operated on a cash economy, Williams felt betrayed. "Has he not received my last let-

A request for a pass for Hiram Smith Williams to enter the city of Mobile and make arrangements for his personal belongings. This pass was issued just before the 40th Alabama Volunteer Infantry Regiment left the city to rejoin the Army of Tennessee in its final efforts to defeat or delay General William T. Sherman in the Carolinas. (Rainwater Collection)

ters, or is he afraid to risk a few dollars"? he asked. The money was critical to his well-being, for "Had I ten dollars in Greenbacks I could get along very well, as I could buy as much clothing and food as I wanted."[33]

The weary monotony of prison life was broken only by the

circulation of wild rumors. Hopeful prisoners repeated dreams of intervention by France, Mexico, England, and new successes by Southern armies. Still others talked incessantly of immediate parole and repatriation. Every small incident or reported incident was open to interpretation, and countless variations were played on the theme of release and return home.[34]

The isolation of the prisoners and their helpless condition made them susceptible to fears about their future, none greater than those generated by the assassination of Abraham Lincoln. Rumors of retaliation for the assassination swept the camp, and the prisoners were forced to live with the possibility that vengeful Federal soldiers would exact a terrible price for the murder of their president. On April 16, the rumor circulated that "3,000 men to be drawn for and shot in this prison as retaliation."[35] When no retaliation occurred, the prisoners turned their attention again to the question of parole.

By the end of July 1865, all prisoners, with the exception of a few Confederate officials, were released from prison. Williams was among the last to leave Point Lookout. His last diary entry on June 6 ends with his wish to be free, "Hope to get out ere long, say in two weeks."[36]

Where Williams went immediately after his release is not known, but within a few months, he was back in Alabama. The travails of the war had not lessened his appreciation for the South, the State of Alabama, or the arts. In 1866, he settled in Demopolis where he established the Demopolis Carriage Company, operated by Reese, Williams and Company, and purchased a large plantation outside the city. In addition to his business activities, Williams was active in the local theater, appearing in no less than three plays during the month of October 1866 alone.[37]

Although initially successful at these ventures, he experienced difficulties in the early 1870s when "the carpet-bag government in Alabama demoralized business, and [he] lost the bulk of his property." While living in Demopolis, Williams wooed and wed Margaret Cornelia Coats, a member of a prominent local family.[38]

Following the failure of his businesses in Demopolis, Williams moved to Selma in 1872. With a partner, David Akins, he established the Selma Carriage Factory and became actively involved in the business of that city. In 1870, Williams and Akins paid E. T. Rhodes $1,500 for the blacksmith and carriage shop they had been renting from him. John Hardy, author of *Selma: Her Institutions and Her Men,* lists him as one of the men of "capital and energy" who were responsible for revitalizing the postwar economy of that city.[39]

In 1873, Hiram S. Williams and his brother, Edmund, visited the Indian River area of Florida. Impressed with the possibilities of the area, Williams went back to Selma and liquidated his business. In early 1874, he moved to the Indian River area and soon became a principal in the founding of the town of Rockledge.[40]

In Florida, he achieved great distinction as a political and civic leader. An ardent Democrat, Williams soon became involved in local politics. In 1875, he became the first postmaster of Rockledge; in 1879, he became the Brevard County treasurer; and, in 1885, he served the first of two terms as a state senator. In addition to his political activity, Williams was a member of the Brevard County School Board.[41]

In Rockledge, Williams practiced his carriage-making trade, but soon expanded his financial interests to growing citrus and other agricultural crops. He found the business success that had eluded him in Alabama, and with increasing prosperity, he became involved in railroad promotion. In 1901, he joined a group of like-minded citizens in establishing the Brevard County Telephone Company, a venture that he served as director and president.[42]

Hiram Smith Williams died November 21, 1921, at his home in Rockledge. His life had spanned almost a century, and he had been a witness to some of the most cataclysmic events of the

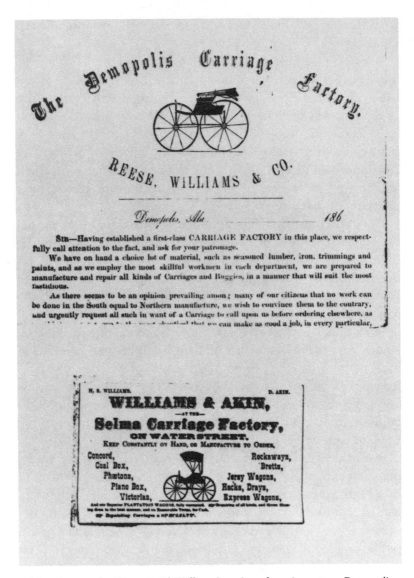

Advertisments for Hiram Smith Williams' carriage shops in postwar Demopolis
and Selma, Alabama (Rainwater Collection)

nineteenth and early twentieth centuries. Always a participant, he was, nevertheless, an astute observer, moved to record his observations in his journals. For that, our understanding of the past has been greatly enriched.

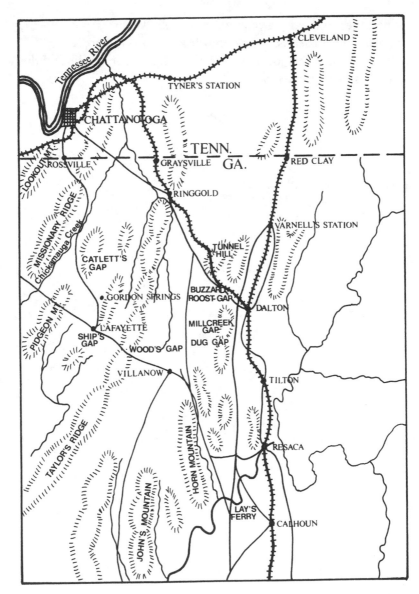

MAP 1.
Dalton to Resaca
FEBRUARY—MAY 1864

# 1

# From Mobile to Dalton

FEBRUARY 16 TO MAY 1, 1864

## Camp Life

A Record of the Georgia Campaign

*By H[iram] S[mith] Williams*

VOLUME 1

### Proem

Miss Mary J[ane] Walker[1]
   Esteemed Friend
   You may remember when I was talking of rejoining my Command in January last that I spoke of keeping a journal, and you requested me to send it to you. I promised you to do so, and I now redeem that promise in part, by sending you the first volume of my record embracing a period of some four months. I trust you will read it with a kindly criticism, for did you but know the circumstances under which the greater part of it was written, you would overlook the faults which I know it must

contain, not only in the style of composition, but also in the lack of skill displayed in throwing the varied incidents together. Seated by my campfire after a long wearisome day's march, I would jot down the events of the day, while a dozen voices around me would tend to draw my attention to other things. But I will make no longer apology for the faults within, knowing that your good sense will overlook them. You will find more to criticize in the penmanship than aught be, but guess at what you cannot read, and when we are meet again I will translate it. With my best wishes for your health and happiness,
Believe me as ever. HSW

## Camplife

_____ *Tuesday. Feb[ruary] 16th, 1864* _____

Two o'clock has arrived. Military power rules, and military orders are imperative. Military power in the shape of three bars of gold lace running horizontally on the collar of a grey coat, says, very politely of course, "Mr. Williams, you must return to your command in the Army of Tennessee."—We remonstrate, very moderately, of course, but gold lace answers our objections by saying with great firmness, "It is absolutely necessary, sir, that every man belonging to that army must be at his post. The country demands it in the first place, and then, more than that Gen[eral Joseph Eggleston] Johnston demands it."2

The straw is placed on that breaks the camel's back. "Gen[eral] Johnston" is the knock-down-argument, conclusive and unanswerable. So we meekly pack our knapsack, put four days rations in our haversacks, bid all our numerous friends, "Goodbye," and march meekly down to the Steamer *Senator* to be transported across the bay. As I said at the commencement, two o'clock P.M. has arrived. The steam whizzes, the engineer turns the wheels two or three times by way of an experiment, the whistle sounds for the last time, a few hurried "good-byes" are spoken, the planks are hauled in, and we are off. I walk the deck in a kind of trance, trying to realize my situation. I look at the city fast fading away in the dim distance. Where am I? Where am I going? The replies are painful enough. The Eastern shore is nearly reached, and now nothing but the spire of Christ's Church is visible. Mobile has faded away from my vision, perhaps forever. The past, the irrevocable past, must henceforth live only in the sweet associations of memory. Farewell to all, to the pleasant places, the theatre, the social hoards. No more must I enjoy the sweet smiles of lovely women or hear their musical voices whispering kind words. The friends I have found must be left and I must go forth again, alone, to fight on in the battle of life. But why dwell here, let me go on and record the few facts that I find worthy the honor.

At Blakeney we take the cars for Montgomery.[3] Two returning soldiers invited me to occupy a seat next to theirs and in their society I passed away the night very pleasantly. Thanks to the kindness of Mrs. Brandt, I have plenty to eat.[4] With true motherly instinct, she stowed away biscuits, potatoes, pies and meat in my haversacks, so that I will not suffer from hunger.

It is just sunrise when we arrive at Montgomery, of a cold morning. Is it because we are farther North, or is it a change in the atmosphere? Yesterday at Mobile it was very warm, today it is bitter cold. It must be the latter. I will not go on now, but wait a day or two as I wish to visit the Theatre here and see some old friends. So the traveling companions I found yesterday must go on without me.

At 10 o'c[loc]k A.M. called at the theatre and was warmly welcomed by nearly all the actors, they thinking I had come up to play. As soon as they were apprised of their mistake, Mr. [Theodore] Hamilton, one of the managers, invited me to his office and invited me to play *Don Jose* in "Don Caesar, the Bazan," to-morrow night.[5] At first refused, but finally consented to play one night. In truth, the weather is so very cold that I had about as lieve stay as not, as I am in no hurry to get up to the Army. So the rest of the day I will study and look about town. The Theatre is much nicer than the one in Mobile. It is larger and much better finished off, while it is far easier to speak.

—————— *Thursday, Feb[ruary] 18th 1864* ——————

I have made my *debut* to a Montgomery audience, and I feel better. Fortunately I felt in excellent spirits tonight. I felt well both bodily and mentally, and I went on to the stage with the same ease that I would walk into a drawing room, filled with old friends. It was Mr. [Theodore] Hamilton's first attempt at *Don Caesar* and he was far from perfect. I never did like to play with Miss [Cecelia] Crisp, but I went through with my part finely,[6] felt the designing and intriguing spirit that must have impelled the original *Don Jose,* providing he had lived, took advantage of the gay, reckless confiding nature of *Don Caesar,* gained the confidence of the beautiful little dancing girl, and just as I was about to reap the rewards of my labors, I disappear from view while my fate was told after by my executioner, *Don Caesar.* The Company here is miserable, all the talent outside of Mr. Hamilton and Mr. [Charles] Morton could be put in a nutshell. What persons go on the stage for who have not intelligence enough to conceive the characters they attempt to personify is what I never could learn. They only make asses of themselves by so doing. Now I should like to remain here two months just to see what I could do. But perhaps the time will come, so to-morrow I will pursue my journey on towards Dalton, with the best grace I can put on the matter.[7]

It is still very cold [and] unpleasant.

—————— *Saturday Feb[ruary] 20th/64* ——————

In Camp—Yes, here I am in camp once more. It seems very natural to me after 16 months out of camp. Left Montgomery yesterday morning at 8 o'clock and reached Atlanta at two this morning; left there at 8 this morning and arrived in Dalton at 4 P.M. and walked out to the camp, a distance of three miles or so N W. All the boys seemed rejoiced to see me, and proved it by crowding into the little cabin where my mess put up, so as to make themselves and everybody else uncomfortable. Told them all the news I had to tell, and composed some, so as to satisfy them [and] get clear of them at the same time.[8]

What a change from the company in which I first volunteered two years ago. [J. J.] Aughe has lost a leg and has gone. [J. A.] Springsteed is gone. [F. M.] Bradley is wounded, a dozen or more are prisoners at the North, while many of them are dead.[9] Their graves are scattered from Dog River all through Mississippi, at Columbus, Deer Creek, and Vicksburg, to this place.[10] Such is war. Three of my old mess are dead, several are wounded and disabled for life, but otherwise all well.[11] A good omen I hope. We now have a Captain that is a gentleman. As much could not be said for our former one, [William Alexander Campbell] Jones, who, thank heaven, has left us for *our* good.[12]

Captain [Thomas M.] Brunson is as clever a man as one can find anywhere, and I do not mind soldiering under him. I am tired and need rest.[13]

─────────────── *Tuesday 23rd 1864* ───────────────

In line of battle with a thousand camp fires blazing around us, I make this record. But first, let me go back a day or two and bring my journal up this far with some system. On Sunday I rested in camp. On Monday I assisted to make a target for our regiment to practice. Just after roll call at night our Orderly Sergeant came around and said the order had just arrived for every soldier to pack his knapsacks and be ready to move at a moments warning. As I had nearly all my things packed, I had but very little to do. An hour or so afterwards the order came to cook two days rations. That kept us busy the rest of the night. We were ready early this morning to march, but the order did not come until three o'clock this P.M.

This portion of Georgia is a succession of bold ridges and mountains running a little East of North, by West of South. The vallies between are generally fertile, and form the only tillable land. The boldest of these mountains is called Rocky Face, half way up the Eastern slope of which my Brigade was camped. A stream called Taylor's Creek runs through between this mountain and one half as high to the North forming a gap through which gap runs the Western and Atlantic R[ail] R[oad]. As the gap forms the only natural passage to the East of Rocky Face Mountain, it is expected that the enemy will attempt a passage thereby.[14] I may remark here that when ordered to get ready to march it was the opinion of all of us, officers as well as privates, that we would retreat, or in the language of Camp, "tute." We were, however, wrong in our conclusions, for after marching down to the foot of the mountain and crossing Taylor's Creek, we were formed in line of battle just to the rear of the smaller ridge North of the R[ail] R[oad], where we now lie with our guns stacked, ready for use at a moments warning. The whole army, comprising some twenty-five thousand men is in a similar position, extending for several miles along the ridges.[15] Our position is to defend the gap before described, together with two or three more Regiments [and] 4 batteries of artillery. If the enemy attempt to come this way, the Angel of Death will be busy.

—————————————— *Wednesday 24th* ——————————————

Behind a rough breastwork of logs, I will attempt to narrate the day's history as far as I am concerned. Fortunately for me, the mess I am in had a lot of bacon and flour on hand, so that we cooked up a lot of biscuit and everybody knows, cold biscuit is decidedly preferable to cold corn bread. The latter is the poorest apology for food I know of.[16] Well, we ate our biscuit and a small piece of bacon this morning when we moved our position to the top of the ridge. The forenoon was passed in comparative quiet, but about noon the skirmishing commenced pretty heavy along our entire line. Two companies from my Regiment are out on picket duty, and I suppose they are in it pretty heavy. Our right seems to be the scene of the heaviest fighting as the musketry and cannon fire is continual over there. A large force of the enemy advanced about four o'clock on the gap when two of our batteries opened on them with such force as to drive them back. As yet the enemy has not opened on us here with artillery, but our time will come before long. Night has brought an end to hostilities. Only now and then a picket firing in the front. It seems to be the general impression that to-morrow will bring on the general engagement. We shall see. It is quite cold to-night and I have made up my bed on the side of a steep hill, so steep I have to stick my heels in to keep from sliding down hill.[17]

_____ *Thursday 25th* _____

The morning opened gloriously. Too fine a morning for men professing to be civilized to be engaged in cold blooded butchery, but then this is *war*. I was up early this morning and after breakfast fixed up my things ready for anything that might happen. The forenoon passed in expectancy. After a cold dinner on corn bread and a little meat (I have saved two biscuit for breakfast to-morrow) we sat down to pass away the time as best we might. Some were reading, some sleeping, some doing nothing, and some playing cards. I was engaged in the latter source of amusement with Lieut[enant John T.] T[erry] and two others, when suddenly whizz—zzz a Yankee shell went over our heads and bursted, scattering a thousand fragments in every direction around us. "Well" said Lieut[enant] T[erry], "I think we had better leave this place," [and] such a scattering I never saw before.[18] Every one sought the friendly shelter of a tree, where I, not to be outdone by *old veterans,* listened to the bursting of shells in fancied security. There is something awful in the bursting of a shell and the shrill hiss of a minnie ball that has to be heard to be fully appreciated. After an hour or so, we were moved down the hill, where we again took up our station. The firing was very rapid and continued until nearly dark. The enemy made a charge on our line and reached part way up the hill, but were repulsed, and two companies of some 20 men each, taken prisoner. Our battery of Parrot guns on the hill done some fine execution, killing a large number of the enemy and wounding many. Some of our Regiment were brought in wounded from picket, but none killed so far.[19]

Most of the afternoon I passed below the ridge reading a book, only dodging every time a shell bursted over me. It is still cold and clear, rather pleasant weather for this kind of life. It is a wonder how well I stand it, much better than I ever expected to do after my life of comfort in Mobile.

To-morrow we will either have a fight or else the enemy will retreat back.

——————————— *Friday 26th* ———————————

The day is passed and I am still alive. Early this morning one of our Captains went up to the top of the ridge and soon returned, saying "Now boys we'll have it. The Yanks are coming in two splendid columns. A most magnificient array." I confess that I began to feel somewhat uncomfortable. As long as I could not see the enemy, I felt a certain sense of security, but now that there was a prospect of meeting them face to face, just the thought caused a tremor to run over me, more than all the shelling of yesterday combined. After waiting some hour or so for them, one of my Lieutenants went up the hill and returned with the rather pleasing intelligence that they had all filed off to our right and had disappeared behind a ridge, some two miles off. The whole day has been devoted to skirmishing, as we have had no general engagement today. I think the main body of the enemy has gone, leaving some skirmishers behind to protect their rear.[20]

This afternoon our line of pickets were doubled with the intention of advancing. We had two days rations in our haversacks and the impression prevailed that we shall advance ere long. I doubt it.[21]

Last night it was very cold and the prospect for to-night is still more dreary. The boys are now in very good spirits, and I think they would make a very good fight now.

To-morrow will decide it.

_____ *Saturday 27th* _____

The Tragedy is over. We are still in line of battle, but will return to camp to-morrow. Now for the events of the day. Last night was the coldest we have had since we have been out. It was so cold that I got up at three o'clock, as I could not sleep. Built a good fire and managed to pass the remainder of the night quite comfortably. The forenoon was passed in quiet, the skirmishing becoming lighter in the distance. Some of our boys came in with some prisoners, who reported the enemy all gone. They have tried our position and strength [and] have returned to get a heavier force no doubt before trying it again. They were under the impression that nearly all our army had gone to Demopolis to reinforce Pope. In that, they were right, but not quick enough, as nearly all the troops sent down there have returned and are now with us.[22]

About 1 o'clock P.M. we received orders to fall in. Done so when orders were given to "Forward March!" On reaching the top of the ridge the valley below us was black with lines of armed men. At least a mile ahead of the column extended regiments and Brigades easily distinguished by their battle flags and bands of musicians. Following the R[ail] R[oad] some time we then took the wagon road and through the dust and dirt pursued our way. After going some three miles we halted for rest. Rested an hour perhaps, then we were "about faced" and back we marched again to our original position. I do not understand the movement nor no one else. It very forcibly reminded me of "Hudibras'" account of a similar movement by a hero of the olden time.[23]

> The King of France and 20000 men
> Marched up a hill, then marched down again

To apply it I have only to alter it thus,

> Our General Johnston
> With 20000 men
> Marched up to Tunnel Hill
> And then, marched back again.

So much for the fight. I have confined myself as you see to the simple facts as they occurred near me. A friend of mine in [Major General Henry DeLamar] Clayton's Brigade has given me a history of their movement which is of much more typical a nature than ours.[24] The heaviest fighting occurred on our right where that Brigade was stationed [and] he tells me that the fighting was severe there for some time. The shell and ball falling like hail about them. On our left there was some heavy fighting too, with severe loss on the part of the enemy. Our men were so well protected by their strong natural positions, that our loss was small compared to that of the enemy.[25]

On our return from our *advance,* we met some of the "Pioneer Corps" who had just finished burying the dead of the enemy. They reported some thirty men in front of our lines near the "gap." At one place one of our shells burst among a squad of the enemy, killing seven of them. One poor fellow had the top of his head blown completely off, and his brains lay scattered on all sides. It was horrible to look on. A grave near the R[ail] R[oad] was marked by a small piece of plank, on which was crudely carved—

"B. C. Garrison, Co K"
"85th Ill. Regt."26

Poor fellows! I would pity the untimely death of the bitterest foe I have on Earth. To think of these men, but a few hours ago in the enjoyment of life and health, now buried by stranger hands. Dieing on the battle-field, with no kind friends to cheer our last moments, it is fearful.

War at best is horrible enough to cause a shudder to chill the heart of all good men, but this [one] so unholy, so bitter, in its progress, so useless as to results, so absurd as to the establishment of any great and vital principle, is the worst record upon the pages of modern history. It makes me mad when I reflect upon it, its cause, progress and the uncertainty of its duration. Like all wars, the innocent have to suffer, the innocent die, innocent hearts break, while the guilty live and prosper, all over the land. I have seen enough in this little affair to make me more deadly opposed to the cursed custom, than ever before.

_____ *Sunday 28th* _____

In camp once more. It seems like home to get back to our cabins, rough and miserable though they are. One does not stop to inquire about the neatness of quarters, after having slept in the open air for a week. Just so that we have a roof over our heads is enough.

We returned to camp this morning before breakfast and passed the rest of the day in writing letters and resting ourselves. If we only had a good supply of rations now we would get along pretty well, but our bacon is all gone, and we have nothing but poor beef and corn meal.27

_____ *March 10th 1864* _____

Quite a long jump from Feb[ruary] 28th up to today, but nothing has transpired of sufficient importance to justify my making a daily entree. Have been out on picket once, [and] been on guard duty once at Camp. Very cold and very disagreeable. A few days ago I was asked if I should like to be detailed in a Pioneer Corps. After some hesitation told them yes. So last night an order was read out on Dress Parade for me to report to Capt[ain John R.] Oliver at the Pioneer Camp situated at the gap, noticed in my description of the battle-field.[28] Came down and found Capt[ain] Oliver to be a very clever gentleman in appearance, and the mess I am assigned too, a very fine one, with large comfortable quarters to live in. There is seven in my mess, of as clever sociable fellows as you would wish to meet with. And then better than all, they are *clean,* a great *consideration* in camp. The rations are a little more plentiful [and] a little better in quality here than at camp.[29]

Well, what have I made by the exchange? A good deal in my way of thinking. First, I have no drill. Secondly, roll call but once-a-day, in camp three times, with all one's accoutrements on. We stand guard here but once in about twenty days, in camp once in every three or four days. To be sure we have to work now and then, but I do not engage in any *battle.*

────────────── *Sunday 13th* ──────────────

The more I see of this Company, the better I like it. All seem to be a clever, sociable set of fellows as I ever met. I can congratulate myself on my good fortune in getting this company.

We have orders to build two dams, so as to overflow the valley of Taylor's Creek and we have to get the lumber at Tilton, a small R[ail] R[oad] station 9 miles below Dalton.[30] We left our camp at Mill's Gap this morning at daylight [and] walked to Dalton (3½ miles) where we took the train and came on to Tilton. Soon after our arrival, we went out to repair the roads so as to haul our stocks to mill. After which I washed [and] put on some clean clothes. Then in company with two of my mess, Mack [probably William McMullen] and Duncan, went down to the river, a good sized stream called Conesoga [*sic*] to cross over.[31] Arriving at the ferry we discovered a skiff half way across with a girl seated in the stern paddling away with a good deal of dexterity, while another was seated in the skiff as a passenger. Looking across the river we beheld a third seated on the opposite bank awaiting the arrival of her companions. "Well boys," said I, "here is a chance for an adventure," and it proved so as the sequel will show. When the boat reached the opposite shore [and] had deposited its passengers, we hailed it. Over it came with the fair ferry girl paddling away as handily as I could have done it. She was of medium size, well formed, passable good looking, dressed very neatly, with a clear black eye that sparkled in its brilliancy. Duncan fell in love with her immediately. We engaged passage at once [and] for the first time in my life I was ferried across a river by a young woman. Romantic wasn't it, on this lovely Sabbath afternoon? I complimented her on her dexterity with a paddle, and apologized for troubling her to take us across, whereupon I learned that she and her sister plied the ferry regularly. This was a new phase in Georgia life. On reaching the opposite shore, I spoke to the two ladies awaiting our arrival, inquired about the country, and a great many other things, just to keep up a conversation. They told us they would return to town to attend church at 3 o'clock and we told them we would return by that time if we could and accompany them. We proceeded on out in the country some two miles, calling at the different houses, when we finally arrived at the house of a widow lady, Mrs. S, who boasted of having three unmarried, but marriageable, daughters on hand. We passed the remainder of the day there, and about dark we left, after having made, as I consider, a good impression.

The youngest daughter, Amanda, is really a pretty girl, rather below medium size, good figure, fine carriage, plump as a young partridge, with very rosy cheeks, and a soft black eye—really I should like to see her in a passion once, just to see those eyes flash. I confess that she made quite an impression on my mind, and I flatter myself that I shall see her often while we stay here as we received a pressing invitation to call again.

There are plenty of girls in this part of Georgia, but very few goodlooking ones. As a general thing, the inhabitants are poor, small farmers, and as nearly all the men folks are gone to the war, they have a poor and hard work to make a living.

—————————— *Monday 14th* ——————————

The day was passed in cutting timber some miles from town. After our return, and before I got supper, the Captain came to me and asked if I did not want to attend a wedding. Told him "yes" of course, tired as I was. Said it was across the river, near the ferry. Thought at once of my ferry maid and wondered if it was her. By the way on yesterday at Mrs. S.'s, I learned their names. There are two sisters, the Miss Dean's, the eldest Miss Mary, the youngest Miss Amanda Jane. I was soon ready and we went down to the ferry where we found some dozen or more awaiting passage. From one of the boys there, I soon learned the particulars of this most strange affair. The bridegroom, Mr. P., was an Arkansas soldier, while the bride was a Miss C., living two miles above Tilton. It seems Shakespeare's maxim that the "Course of true love never did run smooth" was true in this case. The "old folks at home" objected, and a runaway match was the result. As the river is the boundary between two counties, they were leaving one county to be married in another, Murray. When all the party had got across, the loving couple stood up beneath a beach tree on the banks of the swift Conesoga, and were then united in the bonds of wedlock. It was a romantic scene. The moon nearly full was shining through a mass of fleecy clouds, while the crowd beneath the trees looked in the dim-light like weird sisters of the Macbeth era. The squire who performed the ceremony was an old spectacled genius, rough and uncouth as we generally find them in the wild backwoods. With a lantern in one hand, he pronounced the awful ceremony, or rather *awfully* pronounced the ceremony that made the two one. I enjoyed the scene *hugely*. After it was over, all returned across the river but the Captain and myself. We accompanied the Miss Dean's home where we passed a most agreeable evening. Feeling in a good talking humor, I occupied the attention of the old folks and Miss Mary also, while the Capt[ain] devoted his talents to Miss Jane.

_____ *Friday 18th 1864* _____

Tuesday it was very cold. Wednesday ditto, yesterday a trifle warmer. It was about as disagreeable weather as I have seen for a long time, so much so, that I could not muster up courage enough to visit any of my lady friends, until last night when the Captain, Duncan, and myself passed the evenings at Miss Dean's. And a pleasant evening it proved to be. I felt in a glorious humor, and I talked nonsense by the wholesale. Kept all laughing at my remarks until nearly ten o'clock when we returned to Camp. *Memo*: Nonsense is the only kind of talk appreciated or understood by the girls in this neighborhood.

As we had nothing to do today, Duncan and myself concluded we would go hunting. So after an early breakfast, we crossed the river, and after borrowing a rifle with ammunition at Dean's, we started out. This is the pleasantest day we have had this week excepting Monday and Sunday. I wanted to go back in the country some five miles, but Duncan wanted to hunt in the bend of the river [and] so certain was he or pretended to be that he could kill a turkey that he bet me a quart of whiskey we would find one. After wandering through the woods until twelve o'clock, we stopped in a rough log-cabin to get dinner. Had a fine dinner, good corn bread, waffles, ham, sweet and sour milk, molasses, and so forth. Done it full justice, as you may well believe.

As we were tired of hunting, we concluded we would visit some of our female friends and pass the afternoon in that way.

And a pleasant afternoon it proved to be. The girls were in fine spirits, so were we. A soldier has no need of false modesty in these times. He must have plenty of *impudence* if he expects to get along in society now. In fact, a soldier without impudence had better remain in camp altogether and never pretend to pass an hour socially among the softer sex. We had to meet the gold-lace gentry very often, but I think, we generally came off first best. This is one reason why I like this company, if we are anywhere but in the midst of an army, we can visit in the neighborhood and pass away time agreeably.

―――――――――――――― *Sunday 20th* ――――――――――――――

Back in our comfortable old quarters once more. It seems like home to get back, after our Tilton expedition.

We returned last evening about dusk very tired. This morning, soon after breakfast, I went up to the Reg[imen]t to see the boys and to get my letters. Received two bundles of papers from my friend Miss Mary J[ane] W[alker] of Mobile, besides a very interesting letter from her. The papers will assist me to pass away many an otherwise tedious moment. This is a very pleasant day, quite warm and cheerful after our cold spell. It has truly been a day of rest to me, for I am very tired with my hard work down at Tilton, the hardest work I had done for years, much harder than the Theatre.

―――――――――――――― *Tuesday 22nd* ――――――――――――――

Yesterday I worked very hard hewing some timber for the dam. I retired last night early very tired, but could not sleep. Was very restless all night, dreaming some strange dreams. By the way, I will relate one dream that from its singularity made a great impression on my mind. I dreamt I was in Mobile and was engaged in the Theatre. After playing in the first piece with great success, I dressed [and] left the Theatre. A church near there, I suppose it must have been Christ's Church on the corner of

Church and St. Emanuels, was just out. While passing by, I mingled with the crowd and soon a lady and gentleman passed by, followed by a lovely girl of some 16 summers, rather small of her age, but beautiful as a fairy. Just as they passed me a young man went up to her and asked for her company, which she refused. He persisted when the girl turned to me and by her look implored my protection. I advanced to her side. The young man left us in great rage. Then laying her hand on my arm she looked up in my face, and such a look from a pair of large soul-mirrored eyes, and said, "I know you are a Theatre actor, and Ma tells me that actors are bad men, but I know you will protect me by your looks."

"A change came over the spirit of my dreams," as Byron says, and I was walking up one of the streets in the suburbs of the city when my attention was drawn to a large collection of people at a fine residence right and but just before me. Impelled by curiosity, I went in and found it was a funeral and on making the inquiry was told that Mr. McG's youngest daughter had died the night previous. I went to the coffin, and there, beneath a thin gauze shroud, I beheld the face of the lovely girl whose protector I had been. A single white rose was entwined in her hair, but she looked surpassingly beautiful and so deep a feeling pervaded my mind that with a cry of horror I awoke, and for an hour afterward, I lay and thought about this most strange dream.

This morning we found it snowing quite hard, with some two inches on the ground. After breakfast, I sat down by a good fire and wrote for an hour or more, [and] together with reading managed to pass away the forenoon. It snowed very regularly all the forenoon until nearly dark, when it cleared off and the full moon shone on the snow rendering it nearly as light as day. About 12 o'clock we went out and tried to work, but after half an hours labor returned and gave it up as a bad job. Studied Horatio during the evening. It is going to be a very cold night. It beats any weather I ever saw at this time of year in this part of the world.[32]

_____ *Saturday, March 26th* _____

At last we have a pleasant day. On Tuesday last we got up in the morning to see the ground covered with snow as I have before recorded. On Wednesday it nearly all disappeared and we all congratulated ourselves that Spring, so devoutly wished for, had come at last, but in that we were disappointed for the next day it was cold and blustery. Just such a March day as I have seen in more Northern latitudes, while on Friday, we were again greeted with snow. All day long it rained by fits and starts. The snow disappearing and giving way to a worse evil, Mud. I was on guard duty last night so I do nothing to-day, but cook. This guard duty is far more pleasant than in camp. I had to *stand* three hours, from 9 until 12, but as I stand in the house nearly all the time, by a good fire, I did not mind it much. In fact, I had rather do it than work.

We are very busy just now making two dams to throw across Taylor's Creek to impede the progress of the enemy should they again attempt to advance by this route.[33] I find it rather hard work, but I have a good jolly crowd to work with, and then at the worst it is far preferable to soldiering. I like my messmates better and better as I get acquainted with them, and I trust that if I have to remain in the army, I shall stay with this company.

I went up to the Brigade night before last, hoping and expecting to get a package from Mobile, but was disappointed. Do not know when I have felt more sadly disappointed than I was then. But perhaps it will come ere long.

As a general thing I have felt well, both in body and mind since I have been here. The cloudy sensation, so troublesome in Mobile, has nearly left me, leaving my mind clear and active, but to-day I find my ideas are rather dull again. Good health is better appreciated in Camp I believe than anywhere else. Thus far I have certainly been blessed, not having seen a real sick day since I have been in the army.

The shades of night are beginning to come on so I will close this record.

_____ *Sunday March 27th* _____

Sunday in camp! How differently I used to pass them, going to church with some lady friend, eating a good dinner with them afterwards and the passing [of] a social afternoon. But "this eternal blazon must not be" as Hamlet's ghost says. I must forget them, or if I cannot do that, I, at least, must not think of them else I will suffer with a fit of *ennui*. I awoke this morning and heard a little bird singing so sweetly near our cabin that I mused a long time [and] dwelt on old, very old memories, of happier times. Ah me, here I am running off in the very next sentence, in the same forbidden path.

I got up to find a cloudless sky above me, and soon the sun bathed the mountain tops above us in golden light. It is a lovely day, after our week of cold and snow and rain. A pleasant contrast, and I love to dwell upon it. It reminds me of our Country. The past week has been what our Country now is, this day what it will be when Peace smiles upon us again. How the heart of all will rejoice when the dark clouds of war that now hover o'er us, deluging the land with blood, shall have passed away and the glorious sun of Peace bathes us with her golden rays. How I wish the clouds would break now, and let Reason resume her lawful throne among men. But no, no, rivers of blood must yet sweep down the channels of Time ere that blessed day can arrive.

Had a very good dinner to-day for camp. I will give a bill of fare

> White peas boiled
> Piece of Bacon boiled in peas
> Corn-bread
> Bread made out of corn meal

Not much of a variety, but very palatable I assure you to a hungry man. Then we have the very best water to wash it all down with. After we had declared ourselves perfectly satisfied I lit my pipe, and read the Mobile papers recevied yesterday from Miss W[alker]. Studied the ghost of Hamlet and commited every word of it. Quite a good day's work in my opinion.

Also wrote to F. M. Bradley and J. J. Aughe. After supper went up to the Regiment to see a gentleman going to Mobile. Will send a pipe to my "Ma" as a momento of these war times.

Returning I lit my candle and sat down to finish up my journal. It is a warm pleasant Spring-like night, just such as one as I should love to spend in Mobile with my lady friends. How charmingly I could pass away these weary hours. But my path of life lies in a different direction now, and I must journey on until the Great Disposer of all directs differently.

I must go to bed, for we have a hard days work before us tomorrow, and the powers that be say we must be at it by daylight. So let me see what dreams will occupy my mind. Pleasant ones I hope. *Bueona Notchas.*

——————————— *Monday April 4* ———————————

It is a night of clouds of darkness and of storm. All alone by my camp-fire I sit down to make this record. Alone and yet not alone, for the slow measured heavy breathing of my mess-mates tell me that companions are near, though buried in the tranquil oblivion of slumber. I am on-guard to-night, very different from the camp-guard that I used to do, with a gun upon my shoulder, walking my dreary post for two long hours, sow I build me a good fire and sit by it with a book to read, going out and taking a survey every half hour or so.

It has been a long time, very long indeed, since I have attempted to stray amid the flowers of paens. Dare I attempt it now? I will try and put some of my thoughts in rhyme, though I fear they will be rough ones.

> I sit by my Campfire lonely and weary
> For the night it is cold [and] dark and dreary
> I hear the wind in the mountain gorge roaring

I list to the rain in a wild torrent pouring
And I muse on the Present so dark [and] so dreary
As I set by my Campfire so lone and so weary

Weary indeed of a poor soldier's life
Weary of all this mad turmoil [and] strife
Weary of roll-call, weary of drilling
Weary of marching and weary of killing
Weary of labor in sunshine and rain
On breastworks and baricades oft done in vain

I'm weary of standing on guard through the night
And watching the stars as they sink from my sight
And wonder if the next relief is not most near
And watch for the bright morning star to appear
and I'm weary of Picket in sunshine [and] storm
And all the stern duties we have to perform

I am weary of battle, though glory by there
Of winning green laurels for others to wear
I'm weary of seeing my friends mid the slain
Or wounded and writhing in torture [and] pain
Begging for water in heart-rendering tones
and filling the air with sighs [and] with groans

I am weary of hearing the shells burst in air
With a shreik like a fiend in the depths of dispair
I am sick of hearing the balls whistle by
Saying so plainly "I strike [and] you die."
I am weary of war, of powder [and] ball
I am weary [and] sick of the *glory* [and] all

Oh, where are our statesmen [and] have we got one?
To end what our demagogues madly begun
Not one in our land to start into life
With brain and with nerve to stop this sad strife
Alas for our country! Alas for our day!
If we wait for the battle to stop this mad fray

Too much blood has already flowed like a river
Too many fond hearts have been parted forever
Too many farewells with tears have been spoken
Too many fond circles already been broken
Footsore and weary over paths steep and rough
We have fought, we have bled, we have suffered enough

Then pray for this war, so unholy, to cease
Let us pray for the Angel of Mercy [and] Peace
Long banished to come stretch forth his beautiful hand
And dispel the dark clouds that swallow our land
And pronounce that the reign of the Furies is o'er
And bid us like brothers to live evermore

I honestly believe that the above lines contain the real and true sentiments of ninety-nine hundredths of the soldiers composing our armies and at least four-fifths of those out of the army. Yet what newspaper would dare publish them at the present time? What a sad commentary on *Liberty*, on *freedom*. My time is up so I close this record for the night.

——————————— *Sunday April 10th. 1864* ———————————

I have come to the conclusion that Spring will never visit these benighted regions. Sometimes a day or so will be warm and genial, and we will congratulate ourselves that Spring has come, but Alas! for the transitory things of Earth. The next day all our pleasing anticipations are dispelled by a Nor'Wester. This has been a very unpleasant day. Cold, cloudy, but to-night the new moon looks down from the summit of Rocky Face, with rather a smiling countenance.

I have passed the day in my quarters most of the time reading and writing. Wrote to Miss M[ary Jane Walker] this morning and read a bundle of papers received from her on Friday. This afternoon attended a baptizing at the Creek nearby. Seven soldiers were immersed. It reminded me of a scene years ago far away from here.[34]

Went up to the Brigade this evening. Saw the boys. All well, with a few exceptions.

One of my mess-mates left us this evening and another came to take his place, and I do not like it at all. We had a splendid mess as it was [and] I don't like to see it broken up. But we cannot have all things as we wish it here in the army. All the company are in bed, excepting the guards and I, alone am seated at my rude table, making this record. The silence reigning around me is awful. So I will read a little and then "follow suit by retiring."

Later—Have read a little but do not feel like sleeping, so I will fill another page or two. I have been thinking a good deal lately about our present position in the eyes of the world and while viewing the various Brigades composing this Division on inspection this morning, my thoughts took something of this shape. Several centuries ago, before the Southern Confederacy was thought of or the land comprising it was known even to the civilized world, the Supreme Ruler of the Universe appropriated one day in seven for mankind to rest from their labors and worship him. That day is now passed by our military rulers here in inspecting the soldiers, at least the best part of it, from 8 until about 11 o'clock A.M. and sometimes even later. The poor private has to put on his clean clothes, if he is fortunate enough to have any, buckle on his accoutrements, shoulder his gun, and march three-quarters of a mile, form a line of battle, then wait to be inspected by the commanding officers who take their own time to *ride* on the field. What really matters it if one general keeps a thousand or two soldiers waiting for an hour or more of a cold frost morning as their monuments. The private has no right to complain, not at all. Well, that is the way the army spends the Sabbath mornings up here in the army.[35]

A few days ago, Jefferson Davis appointed a day for Fasting and prayer.[36] It came on Friday last and strict orders were issued for all soldiers to observe it faithfully. No work, no duties to be performed and all were requested to "Fast" during the day or until four o'clock P.M., then they could eat up all their rations at one meal. Of course the "Fasting" part was the subject of much ridicule by the boys who *fast* every day if they depend on the Government rations alone for daily food. The day came and passed. It was religiously observed throughout the army. No drilling. No work on fortifications, and no three hours "inspection." Now who has been the most power and who is most readily obeyed—the Creator of the world or the President of the Confederacy?[37]

What consistency. What faithful obedience to the powers that be.

I am getting sleepy now.

—————————— *Monday April 18th '64* ——————————

This has been a day long to be remembered by me. But first let me glance over the events of yesterday. It proved to be a lovely day, only cool for this time of year. Wrote to Miss W[alker] in the forenoon and read Miss [Mary Elizabeth] Braddon's novel *Aurora Floyd.*[38] I cannot say that I admire it altogether, although to state my objections would take more space and more time than I care about devoting to it. There is much good sound practical common sense in it, many trite sayings, while the character of *John Mellish* is extremely well drawn. *He is* the hero of the book. His broad, good humored face makes an impression on one that will endure for years. Aurora's character is well drawn, but I cannot admire her as a woman. No honorable highminded woman would ever marry a man, even though she honestly believed herself to be a widow, without telling him of her first marriage. What can be more dishonorable than such a deception, for a widow to marry a second time as a maid. Bah!

Mr. [Lucius] Potter visited me in the P.M.[39] Passed a very pleasant afternoon in smoking, talking and roaming about these romantic hills, listening to the birds singing and plucking the early spring flowers.

Towards night it rained. A slow, cold, dismal rain, but as we have a good roof over our heads, we smiled at the inclemency of the weather and sought our limbs to be soothed to refreshing slumber by the pleasant patter on the roof. Oh, what glorious childish memories came sweeping across the vista of the past as I listen to "the rain upon the roof." How many a night I have been soothed to the sound sweet sleep of boyhood by the rain, and how well I remember it, in the dear, delightful place that ever has been, and ever will be, *home.*

Yet I was not destined to undisturbed sleep. I felt unwell and passed a restless night. My nervous system seemed to be out of order [and] I could not sleep. Add to this fact that I ate too much dinner yesterday. It is astonishing what an appetite one gets up here among the hills. I eat as much at one meal as I used to eat in Mobile all day. And I never enjoyed better health. I have had no symptoms of dyspepsia since I have been here. Very pleasant record.

Now let me tell you why this day will be long remembered by me.

First let me tell something about my mess. It consists of 6 persons, and the head of the mess is a tall 6 foot 4 speciman of a pin[e]y woods genius from South Ala[bama]. Good natured and jovial as you ever find them. As he is the oldest man we all call him "dad" while he designates us as his "gals." He has three single ones. *Jane, Sal,* and *Amanda,* the last cognomen being the one he gave me. The two married ones is Mrs. Green and Mrs. Hedgepet. We have rare old times now and then, and "dad" has a hard time to keep his gals straight. Well, *Dad* had remained at the quarters doing the cooking for the past two weeks, and as I was tired of working on the dam, I proposed to change with him, which proposition he accepted, and consequently went out to work this morning while I remained at the quarters.

Was busy getting dinner over, when our Commissary Sergeant, returned from H[ea]d Q[uarters] and handed me a letter. I glanced at the superscription and saw it was from my kind friend Miss W[alker] of Mobile. So I set down and broke the seal with a good deal of anxiety, for her letters are always interesting to me. On taking out the letter I found it was not in her handwriting, and a second glance told me it was my brother's.[40] It was a glorious letter, reminding me of "old times" and I read it with a good deal of pleasure as one may well imagine. All alive at home and well, excepting mother.[41] No one can form a correct statement of the pleasure one feels to hear from the *loved ones at home*, until he has been deterred from that privilege by the armed hand of war as I have for the past three years. Yet there is a sadness connected with it that reminds me of what the poet says, "there is no joy without a sting," "no rose without a thorn," and the question is asked, "When are you coming home?" Alas! When indeed?

Great changes have taken place in that hallowed spot, and all around the haunts of my boyhood. Men, who were my playmates at school, have been killed on the battle field. Girls, I cannot help but call them girls still, have been married and become mothers. Verily, ten years work great changes.

Went up to the Reg[imen]t after dark and calling on my friend, the Doctor,[42] he handed me a bundle from Miss M[ary Jane Walker] containing two papers, one pocket hankerchief, a lead pencil and a half-round file. They were acceptable, especially the led [*sic*] pencil. It also contained a circular of brother's and I should judge he was doing a very good business in the nursery line. How I should like to pass a week or two with him about the time fruit begins to get ripe. It is too pleasant to think about. Sat up until about ten o'cl[oc]k reading and talking to W[illiam "Billie"] McMullen, who lived within a few miles of my home in N[ew] J[ersey] and was acquainted with several persons there that I used to know. It is pleasant to talk with such a one at this time.[43]

————————— *Tuesday April 19th/'64* —————————

After a hard days work I sit down to make this record. And what you ask, have I done so hard to-day? Something the soldier

dreads and detests more than all else, if I am a standard. *ugg.*
Attended a review of the whole army. We received orders to get
ready this morning by eight o'clock and we were ready by that
time. Half the company are down at Tilton getting lumber so we
could not make much of a show with our spades, picks [and]
axes. First marched to Gen[eral Alexander Peter] Stewart's
H[ead] Q[uarters], then after forming the division, we marched
on down below Dalton in all about four miles from here.[44] It
was cold and very disagreeable. Add to which the wind blew a
gale at times, raising the dust so as to shut objects from view
across the street. There was a large turnout, and I think Gen[eral
Joseph E.] Johnston must have got tired of it before it was over.
At all events I got tired before our Division passed by, which
was I think the 3rd and there was four more yet to pass. We
returned to camp about two o'clock or later, tired [and] weary
with our tramp.[45]

Nothing tires me out sooner than this marching with a company. Let me walk by myself [and] I can get on well enough, but
there is a great difference between *walking* and *marching*. Ate
dinner and supper combined, then rested the rest of the day. It is
going to be a cold night. The *ghost* in *Hamlet* could "scent the
morning air." I can scent the active campaign about to begin.

I have dreamt some strange dreams, like everybody else I
suppose. I have recorded one, and last night I dreamt another. I
remember some time ago, it may be years for I have no recollec-
tion of time past since then, I dreamed that I was composing a
poem on some subject, now forgotten, [and] I composed verses
of correct rhythm and rhyme. Woke up and they were so vivid
on my mind that I repeated them, [and] thought that I would
write them down the first thing in the morning, but when morning came, I could not recall a line. Well this dream of last night
was of a similar nature. Whether I dreamed it was actually
happening or whether I was writing a story I do not know, but
here it is—

On the Mississippi River a wealthy planter resided, living in
all the luxury and ease that wealth can bestow. He appeared to

be about thirty-five years of age, yet he might have been forty-five, for he possessed that appearance which we sometimes see when ten years in the prime of manhood makes but little change for the worse. His home, situated on the western bank of the "Father of Rivers" overlooking that great stream, was hidden in the foliage of live-oaks and china-trees and there he lived, surrounded by everything calculated to make a man happy, with one exception, a wife. How it was that he had lived to the age of "old bachelordom" without choosing a partner for life was a wonder and mystery that his nearest neighbors and dearest friends had tried in vain to solve, but without success. He possessed all those traits that are calculated to please the fair sex, he could dance, sing, and play, while his manners were polished and agreeable. Showing that he had mixed much in the circles of refinement and intelligent society. Add to all these, his fortune and it was clear to all penetrating minds that the cause of his "single blessedness" lay at his own door.

In truth there was not a mother within his circle of acquaintances, [and] it was by no means small, but had presented their marriageable daughters in the fond hope that their charms might tempt him to take the marriage vows, but alas! Poor souls, Their hopes and their designings were all in vain. Yet in truth, our bachelor friend wanted to marry. For years, he had sought with eagerness for a wife that would prove to him a companion and a friend, but never had he found one that would stand the test of his acute penetration. And as he lived on enjoying life and still looking and longing for the chosen one to appear, and she did appear. It was in this wise as my dream had it.

In the Spring the Mississippi is subject to overflow. The spring of which I write, and I have no idea what Spring that was, the river rose to an unprecedented height, overflowing the bottoms to a greater extent than was put down in the recollections of the "oldest inhabitant." My bachelor friend, one pleasant afternoon when the river was still rising, concluded he would take his skiff and paddle over the vast expanse of water through the thick cypress swamps, partly for curiosity and partly for hunting purposes. So placing his rifle before him, he took his paddle and pushed away from the bank. He thought he was merely going to seek game, but in truth he was going to seek and find his wife. Strange, but nevertheless true.

On through the tangled swamps over bottom lands that had been cleared and cultivated he passed his way. Now and then stopping at a ridge that appeared out of the water, on which the game with which the woods abounded had taken refuge.

I might fill pages of this little volume with a history of his exploits, killing a turkey [and] a deer now and then, but in truth I do not know whether he even saw one or no. But ere long his attention was drawn to the roof of a cabin that appeared out of the water and towards it he paddled his skiff. The water had risen half way to the eaves, and on looking within he discovered traces of furniture that showed plainly that it had been deserted in great haste by its occupants.

While he was busy making his observations and wondering what had become of the family, providing one lived there, he was startled by the cry of a babe not far distant. Seizing his paddle he hastened toward the point from whence the cry proceeded. Not far distant he saw a ridge still some two feet out of the water, and on the highest point, he discovered a human form. Sending his skiff noiselessly through the water, he approached the spot undiscovered, when he witnessed a scene that would have made a stout heart weep. Kneeling upon the ground was a woman and she appeared strangely beautiful with her hands clasped together. Her large brilliant eyes turned toward heaven while her lips moved in silent prayer. Only now [and] then she murmured distinctly, "Oh God, have mercy." Her hair in raven tresses fell to her waist, while her scanty dress revealed a bust of dazzling whiteness and beauty. Before her, wrapped up in a shawl, was a young babe, whose cry had just called the attention of our friend.

Stepping lightly on shore he approached the mother with a noiseless tread. Her eyes were still fixed upward. When he reached her side [and] she said, "Oh Heavenly Father, if I must perish save my child." "Your prayer is answered," said our hero as he knelt down by her side and raised the babe in his stout arms. With a cry of joy that cannot be described she arose to her feet [and] staggering forward, would have fallen if he had not supported her. After seeing them both safely stowed in his skiff, he paddled home where his precious charges were properly cared for. A few words explained affairs satisfactorily. She was a widow living in the cabin before spoken of. Her husband had died 6 months before, since which time she had maintained herself until the great freshet, when she was awakened at midnight by the water running in her door. Seizing her babe and a shawl, she started out and after much difficulty gained the top of the ridge. When daylight came, what was her dismay to find the water surrounding her on every side, shutting off every avenue of escape. There the whole day she remained, watching the water as it rose higher and higher each moment. Who can tell the agony she endured during those long dreary hours. Of course in due time, my bachelor friend married her [and] lived happily ever after.

_____ *Sunday May 1st 1864* _____

I have neglected my journal lately, for the reason that I have not felt like writing.

The first of May has dawned upon us, the day celebrated in the "good old times of yore" when Peace—blue-eyed Goddess—blessed us with her presence,—celebrated with festivals in which the young and old joined. When the Queen of the occasion was crowned with flowers, and worshiped by the assembled crowd as one worthy of homage. But now, we bow down to Mars, the savage God of War, instead of crowns of flowers and myrtle leaves, we weave a chaplet of sighs and groans, and, crown a ghostly skeleton and bathe our brows with blood from the hearts of our friends and brothers.

At last I can write [that] Spring has come. Here are some verses which I humbly present as an offering to her shrine.

> The song-birds with their matin lay
> The wild bee with its ceaseless hum
> Proclaim through all the live-long day
> The joyful tidings—"Spring has come."
>
> I see her in the verdant fields
> With dainty step and graceful mien
> I see the sceptre that she wields
> To clothe the wood in living green.
>
> I pluck the violets on the banks
> Reclining on the velvet sod
> And humbly raise my silent thanks
> From Nature up to Nature's God.
>
> The violets with merry glee
> From far off fountains gayly come
> Fit types of youth and liberty
> And join the chorus, "Spring has Come!"
>
> Oh glorious season for the free
> You find me bound with whose strong hard bands
> Would I could say that Peace [and] thee
> Had come together hand and hand.
>
> More glorious than the unclouded sun
> More lovely than the verdant field
> Brighten the works but just begun
> And with all the glories that you yield
>
> "grim visaged war" with haughty frown
> Proclaims his stern imperious sway

We have the flowers to weave the crown
But not the lovely Queen of May.

Sweet Goddess of the flowery vale
Sweet Spirit by the Zephyr's bourne
We only hear the orphan's wail
And her pale widows as they mourn.

The sweet-mouthed morning wakes
And paler grows the myriad stars
The silence deep-mouthed cannon breaks
Man's offering to the war God, Mars.

Oh, Spring! with all your lovely train
With song of birds and wild bees hum
For joy to us, they sing in vain
The glorious tidings, "Spring has Come."

Somehow all that I write, all that I think takes but one channel; one wish—for this war to end. When will it cease? I ask myself that question a score of times a day, and it provokes me to think that with all our boasted intellect, our great learning, none can answer it.

I think less and less of our boasted civilization every day. In what aspect are we better off to-day than the Romans or Greeks were two thousand years ago. Are we happier? No. And yet the happiness of mankind is the great bubble that we all grasp for, the philosopher's stone we have sought for ages.

On Friday morning last the enemy made a demonstration on our front, and the consequence was that our Division were soon in line of battle, but nothing serious came from it. After a little skirmishing in which we lost two or three men, the enemy fell back to their original positions.[46] This trifling affair affected me very materially in this wise. It caused us to get two days rations of cold corn-bread on hand. *Cold corn-bread,* bah! It is the nearest nothing to eat of anything I ever saw yet. It causes me to lose my appetite everytime I look at the adamantine loaves. I would not ask for a better weapon to knock a man down with than a pone of it—it is equal to a brick-bat.

All is reported quiet up in front just now, but for not long.

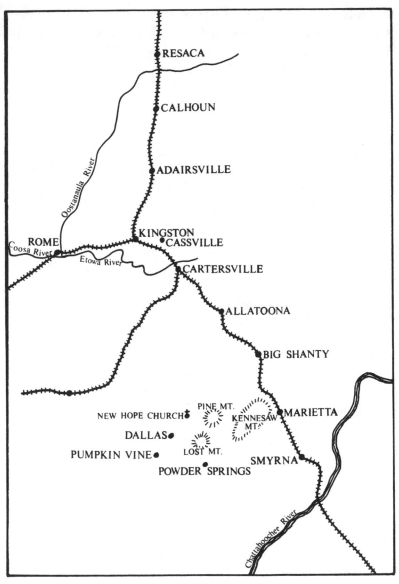

MAP 2.

Resaca to Marietta

MAY–JUNE 1864

# 2

# Prologue of the Great Battle

MAY 7 TO MAY 13, 1864

_____ *Saturday May 7th* _____

The tragedy commenced this morning early.[1] Just after sun-rise we were off for duty mounting one of the high ridges. Here we commenced cutting the trees and underbrush away from before our batteries, when we heard the rattle of musketry to our front, while soon the roar of cannon showed that it was more than an ordinary skirmish. As soon as we finished our job at that point we received orders to go to the front and after our cavalry had fallen back across the bridge over Taylor's Creek, we were to cut it down. This was anything but a desirable job, as one can easily guess, for the bridge was very much exposed and we expected to be fired upon by the enemie's pickets. We went however with a hearty good will. On arriving at the bridge, we found [Major General Joseph] Wheeler's Cavalry crossing in a continuous stream. Crossing the creek, we ascended a bald knob a little distance from which we could easily see the enemy, marching upon a bald hill some mile-and-a-half off, near Tunnel Hill. For two hours we watched them, with their battle flags, looking like little hankerchiefs, while we could see the signal corps waving their signal flags to those in the rear. Returning to the bridge, the last of the cavalry crossed over. When Gen[eral]

Wheeler and his escort passed and ordered us to cut away the bridge. "Hurry up boys," said one of his men, "the Yanks are not over half-a-mile up there."[2]

You ought to have seen us work just then. We had two bridges to cut away, and after an hour's work, we completed the job. We then fell back to a gap between the ridges to our left, where we were to cut the timber across the road to impede their progress and stop their artillery. Cutting the trees half down, we then cut underbrush for our artillery to play in some open fields, which kept us busy until dark. We then returned to our quarters tired and weary, hoping to get a good night's sleep. But in this we were disappointed for about 11 o'clock we were called up and ordered to go out [and] cut the trees down at the gap above spoken of. After three hours hard work we cut all the trees, obstructing the road well, when we returned to our quarters again.[3]

_____ *Sunday May 8th* _____

This has seemed like anything but Sunday to me. We were out early again this morning cutting timber, which kept us busy until eleven o'clock. Returning to our quarters, I went down to the pond and took a good bath. Put on some clean clothes, and felt much better. Wrote a letter to Miss W[alker] and had but finished it, when orders were given to "fall in." Had to go and assist some artillery to get on the top of Buzzard Roost. Had a hard time of it. When on the top of the mountain, we had a fine view of the field below us. The enemy's skirmishers were advancing across the fields in plain view. Directly they crossed the creek and entered an old cornfield where each one took a stump and commenced firing at our skirmishers. It was a grand sight, and I could have looked for hours at them had not other work interfered. We worked very hard at the road until nearly dark when we returned again to our quarters. I learn that my Reg[imen]t was put out on skirmish this morning, when one of our boys was instantly killed.[4]

The enemy have been feeling for our forces all day and I presume the great battle will commence to-morrow. There was heavy firing down to our left some 6 miles, and I now learn that they made three desperate charges but were repulsed each time. As I am very tired I will retire in hopes to get a good night's rest.[5]

—————————————— *Monday, May 9th* ——————————————

The battle is now raging along our entire line, not general, but pretty heavy. As I write the roar of cannon, the shrieking of ball and bursting of shell, makes these old hills echo over and again, while the musketry keeps up a continuous rattle. Most of the firing I think is from the enemies lines.[6]

It is a lovely day, warm and cloudless. Too lovely for such a fearful tragedy as is now being enacted around me. Of course, I can hear a hundred rumors, but I place no dependency in any of them. So I will not occupy space to write them down. We are still in our old quarters, pretty well protected I think, but we may be ordered away from here at any moment.[7]

—————————————— *Night* ——————————————

After writing the foregoing, I put up my writing materials and sat in front of our cabin taking interest. The shells from the enemie's guns flew harmlessly over our heads, bursting sometimes directly over us and scattering the fragments in every direction. Soon a piece of shell fell in front of our quarters and directly another entered one of our cabins, tearing one end out and creating a great havoc generally. Fortunately no one was hurt by it, but it had such an effect on us that our Captain concluded to hunt for safer positions. Packing our knaps[acks] we started across the valley with the ball and shell, whiz-iz-ing over our heads and falling on every side of us, but we reached a position beyond their range, in safety. The spot selected by our Captain is a little valley in a small undergrowth of timber, about half-a-mile from our line of battle. It is a lovely day, clear and very warm, so that it made me perspire very freely coming over here. I am now writing this page laying down on my blanket with my book before me. Far from a pleasant or comfortable position to write in as my handwriting will abundantly testify. The battle is still raging fiercely. The enemy making repeated charges on our works, their endeavor being to get possession of Rocky Face M[ountain]. I judge they are repulsed by the loud cheering, or rather yelling of our boys. Orders have just come in for us to go up on the line of battle to repair some parapets. I expect we will work all night.[8]

──────────── *Tuesday May 10th 1864* ────────────

Another day of blood and strife. Enough to make angels weep over the fallen natures of mankind.

We had to go to our old quarters last night after some tools, but not finding them, and hearing someone digging just above [us] on a hill, we went up there. Found it was a few men from [Lieutenant Thomas J.] Perry's Battery digging a grave for a comrade killed by a shell.[9] His mangled corpse was the awfulest sight I ever beheld. The shell struck him in the side, tearing out the whole stomach from his heart down. His entrails were torn completely to pieces. Poor fellow. He never knew what hurt him for his death must have been instantaneous. Such a sight it seems to me would make every advocate of men possessing human feelings curse the barbarous custom. Taking what tools we could get, we went up on the ridge where I once lay in line of battle for several days and commenced digging on some parapets.

Found my Reg[imen]t but as my company was out on picket, I did not see any of the boys. Only one man thus far had been killed in it. Finishing our work there, we went to our front line half a mile farther to the left and in front where we threw up a rifle pit. Day broke when we got it finished and although the enemy's skirmishers were but a hundred yards or so off, they did not fire at us.[10]

Returning to our camp, I ate breakfast then lay down to sleep, but just as I got good and sound, it commenced raining when we had to put up a shelter. It is anything but pleasant to be camped out in such weather, consequently I have passed anything but a pleasant day.[11]

The fighting to-day has not been as heavy as yesterday, but the cannonading has been more regular, and I judge by the ambulances passing out to the hospitals that there has been more wounded and killed.[12]

It is night once more. A night of clouds and storms. Thank Heaven the fighting has ceased for a time and the tired soldier, even if he cannot sleep, can at least feel that he has a short respite from danger.[13]

The "news" is very cheery. The surrender of [General Frederick] Steele to Gen[eral Sterling] Price with 9000 men. Gen[eral Richard] Taylor beseiging [General Nathaniel] Banks in Alexandria, L[ouisiana]. Gen[eral Robert E.] Lee whipping Gen[eral Ulysses S.] Grant in Virginia and taking a great number of prisoners—two major generals [and hundreds and hundreds]. *Memo. Good news* always comes before a fight.[14]

_____ *Wednesday May 11th* _____

The clouds, rising in inky masses over the western mountains, warned us to look out for a terrible storm, while the thunder vied with the roar of our artillery during the day.[15] Soon after laying down it commenced raining and ere long it poured down accompanied by vivid flashes of lightening and a heavy wind. The wind blew the rain in under our miserable apology for a roof—a blanket stretched over a pole—while the hill-side on which we slept was so steep that we had to stick our heels in the ground to keep from sliding down.[16] Add to this we had but two blankets. One to sleep on and one for our tent, so that we had no covering. More than all, the rain ran down the hill with such force that it filled and ran over our little ditch, wetting our blanket through and making me feel so uncomfortable that I could not sleep a wink. It was an awful long night, and towards morning I got so cold that I had to get up. The rain had ceased, and the stars were shining, but as I had no way to start a fire, I went over to a building near here where some soldiers were sleeping and there found a good fire, by which I sat till morning. Returning to camp, I cooked some batter cakes for breakfast which proved very palatable. I then lay down and took a nap, but ere long, I was disturbed by the very disagreeable cry— "Fall in."

Our lower dam had washed away early this morning and we had to go to the ford just below to clear away the driftwood that had lodged there, obstructing the passage of teams.

It was not a very safe place, as the minnie balls were flying about us pretty thick, and they caused us to pitch in with so much energy that we done the work in a short time, when we returned to camp. It is a miserable day, cloudy with a little misty rain now and then.

I learned that our whole Regiment are out on skirmish this morning, and Capt[ain Ed] Marsh was killed.[17] I am anxious to learn if any of my old friends are injured.

—————————————— *Night* ——————————————

After writing the above, I went over to the Division Hospital to see if I could learn any news from the Brigade or find any of the boys. Found none however as the wounded are taken off to the hospital as soon as their wounds are dressed. Returning to camp, I prepared a place to sleep in as the night is going to be very cold. About ½ past 5 this evening, the firing shots of cannon and musketry was heavier than at any time during the battle. It was one continuous roar for more than an hour, when it died away and about dark ceased altogether. I have since learned that the enemy made three desperate charges on Rocky Face M[ountain], but were repulsed each time. The slaughter must have been very great, else the firing very poor.[18]

I am anxious to learn the list of casualties.

It is still cloudy and threatens rain. I fear another bad night. It is so cold that I can only feel comfortable by the side of a good fire. Strange fact for May in this southern state.

_____ *Thursday 12th of May* _____

We had the glorious satisfaction of seeing the sun rise this morning, while the few clouds remaining of yesterday's storm were broken and flying before the refreshing breeze.

Add to this we have had a day of comparative quiet up to one or two with no firing of any moment were heard. About that time some of our cannon opened on both the ridges on either side of the Rail Road, and continued for an hour or two. The silence was ominous of some important event, and about sundown, we learned that such was the case as we received orders to pack up and be ready to start. Where? that was the question. It did not take much prophesying to answer. Rumors of the enemy forcing a passage through Sugar Creek Gap, some miles below this told the tale.[19] About 9 o'cl[oc]k the order was given—Attention—March—and away we went towards Dalton. A night march, have you any idea what it is like? On reaching the main road we found it strung with wagons and troops all marching to the rear. The truth of the report that the enemy had flanked us to our left was verified.[20] After reaching Dalton we rested until 12 ocl[oc]k. Then at the head of our Division we commenced our night march for Tilton. I felt in very good spirits and got along very well, but soon I got wearied and my feet began to get sore. Over rough causeways, extending through swamps for miles, across creeks and through deep forests, we went on our way and just at daylight we reached the Conesoga River a mile above Tilton.[21] Reached Tilton just at sunrise and put up as I was in hopes for the day. Ate breakfast and lay down for sleep, but just then got orders to repair a ford. Went and fixed it, after two hours work, then returned to camp and went to sleep. Slept for an hour or so when orders came to repair the roads south of this. Went to work on them and after getting a mile or so from town, found that all the army were leaving [and] unless we looked sharp we would get cut off.[22] Returned for our baggage, and found when we reached town that the rear guard of our army had just entered town. Heard the firing of our cavalry some two miles from the place. Shouldered our baggage and started down the Rail Road, until we came to the Resaca wagon road, where we struck off. Every bad place we had to repair in the road and then march on rapidly to get ahead of the wagon train. The road was lined with artillery and ordnance trains, all pushing ahead, while the enemy's cannon to our right told that they were ready for the fight.[23]

At dark we were within a mile of Resaca, a small R[ail] R[oad] town on the Oostanaler river.[24] Ate a hasty supper, but ere I could get done, the order was given—Attention! And as usual with our Captain, it was all spluteration until he was off. Throwing on my things in a great hurry, I started off after them, just catching a glimpse in the dark of one of our boys, as I thought, but the road was lined with soldiers in small squads, so that I soon lost sight of him. Hurrying on I reached the town, but found no signs of the Company. There were three bridges across the river. On wagon bridge, one R[ail] R[oad] and one pontoon bridge. Went to each one of them but no Pioneer Co[mpany] had crossed there. Knowing it to be useless to attempt finding them at that hour, I determined to cross the river and camp for the night among the wagons for I was very tired. Crossed at the pontoon bridge and after crossing the bottom on the opposite side I stoped with some cooks and after smoking went to sleep. The enemy have batteries planted so as to shell the town and my new found comrades told me long stories of their firing and its effect. Several had been killed and wounded during the afternoon. One mule had been struck by a shell which exploded tearing the rider as well as the animal to pieces.[25]

The Conesoga River running South empties in to [the] Eustanola about a mile above here, which then runs west, thus forming a square elbow. Our line of battle as now formed runs across this elbow, the left resting on the Eustanola about a mile below the village, while the right rests on the Conesoga some two miles or more above.[26]

All is bustle and confusion. Wagons going to the rear, cooks busy in cooking corn bread, soldiers cheering one another all indicating tomorrow we will fight.

# 3

# The Great Battle: Atlanta

MAY 14 TO JUNE 19, 1864

_____ *Saturday, May 14th 1864* _____

I was up pretty early this morning and sat by the fire smoking
when I saw one of my company who got lost from us at Tilton
approaching. Hailed him and after telling my story we concluded we would hunt the company together. Went back some
half-mile to the wagons where I got a good breakfast, after
which I lay down and slept for an hour or so. Then, as the
wagons were ordered to the rear still farther, we started for
town. Cannonading was going on at a pretty high rate, while the
small arms had just commenced rattling. Reaching the R[ail]
R[oad], the bank across the bottom afforded us a good shelter
from the enemy's shells. Crossing the Pontoon bridge we crossed
the town and struck off to the right of our line of battle where I
learned our Division was stationed. We soon learned that the
Company had crossed the river, and on reaching it, found the
bridge had broken down some half-hour before. Some fifty men,
however, were at work on it [and] so I sat down and waited
patiently for it to be completed.[1]

The Hospital for our Corps were established across the river,
but as the ambulances could not cross they established temporary ones on this side. In the meantime the firing grew heavy in

on our right, and soon the wounded began to come in. I watched the surgeons cutting off limbs and dressing wounds until I grew sick, then set down on the bank of the river until the bridge was done when we crossed over. Found our company making shelters for our brigade hospitals.[2] In the meantime the battle waxed hotter—one continuous roar of musketry and artillery. We finished the hospitals just before dark, when we went to our old home near us and camped for the night. It was once a beautiful place. A gentle knoll overlooking a broad, rich bottom, while a large peach orchard near us was loaded with young fruit. The moon was shining bright from and unclouded sky, and all nature was covered in repose—we could only hear the dull report of a musket now and then, with the crys and shrieks of our wounded from the hospitals, as the poor fellows underwent the painful operation of having an arm or leg amputated.[3]

## Sunday May 15th

Our boys, just at sunset last night, charged the enemy and drove them some mile or more, when they returned and took up their old position, resting on their arms all night. This morning they found the enemy facing them again ready for battle.[4]

After an early breakfast, I went down to my brigade hospital to dig a hole for the limbs amputated during the fight. Found several of our boys wounded and among the rest my old messmate and friend, Henry C. Harris, who was shot through the lungs, as I fear mortally.[5]

There were two of the enemy also, brought in shot through the body. One was in the last agonies of death and as he died soon after we dug his grave and burried him just at the edge of the forest near the river bottom. I took a piece of plank and crudely carved his name and Reg[imen]t. thereon—"I. Corlist, 51st Reg[iment] O[hio] V[olunteer] I[nfantry]." I placed it at the head of his grave. Poor fellow to die so young, and so far from home.[6]

Returning to camp, I lay down to read myself to sleep, but just as I was about accomplishing my object, I was started up in rather a singular manner. Suddenly we heard a few shots fired above us, and soon a dozen or more of the sick from a hospital farther to our right came running by, crying "the Yankees are coming. Run quick or you will all be captured." Getting up, I put up my things, while my partner, W[illiam] McMullen, threw on his things and started off, leaving me alone, for when I looked around me, I found every man gone. As I had no arms, I concluded to hunt for a secure place. Getting on my own things, I picked up a knapsack coat and haversack belonging to one of my mess-mates and started for the river. Such a scene as presented itself than I never witnessed before. The woods and fields were filled with men on a regular *skedaddle*. Doctors and officers mounted on horses running apparently for dear life. Nurses, sick men, wounded men, all in one confused mess, lining the whole path. As I passed along I saw knapsacks, haversacks, guns, cartridge belts, blankets, in fact every thing that belongs to the soldier's outfit, all scattered right and left. I could not help smiling for all it might be a serious business to me. Reaching the river, I sat down in a secure place to rest. I soon saw my messmate Allen Simmes, whose knapsack I had, and calling to him told him to come up and get his things. As some of the things were still left, I went back to camp with him to get them. On arriving there found everything quiet.[7]

The enemy, magnified to a whole Brigade by our boys, proved to be only a hundred cavalry or so, on a raid to discover our strength there, but as soon as they found it was the hospitals, they burned a few wagons and then retreated. Our cavalry and a few infantry came over to drive them back, but found nothing to do. Two of the enemy were captured however. We now have to move to the rear and fix up some more hospitals. The battle is still raging with terrible fury, if we can believe the reports of the wounded and the rattle of artillery.[8]

My feet are so sore that every step I take inflicts great suffering to me, but shouldering my things, I started out. Crossing the Conesoga we passed through Resaca, over the pontoon bridge, and across the bottom beyond the Eustanala, all the time exposed to the enemy's guns. Reaching the woods beyond, we sat down to rest and wait until the wagons came up, so as to find out where we were to go. Here we found that the "skedaddle" had had its effect, for the cooking wagons had gone, and the cooks in their hurry had left hundreds of pones of corn bread already cooked. We all filled our haversacks, and after eating our dinner, we passed our way four miles from the river on the railroad where three trains had stoped to take on the wounded. Here we were to remain for the night. What a scene—hundreds of ambulances filled with wounded men, the road lined with stragglers, litter carriers and hospital nurses. All mingled up in one core to entangled confusion.[9]

We pitched our camp near by, in a young growth of pine timber, where we proposed to spend the night, when indeed we are disturbed before morning.

Here we can see what war is in all its horrid and distable qualities.

_____ *Monday May 16th* _____

How shall I describe the past night? If I live to the allotted period of man's existence, I can never forget the scenes I have witnessed for they are indelibly stamped on my memory. Limbs mangled and torn, much suffering and pain—Oh, Lord! It was truly horrible. About two o'clock last night we were ordered to assist our Division Surgeons about getting the wounded men on board the train bound for Atlanta. The wounded for the whole Corps were scattered about on every side. Some in a deserted house, some under rough shelters of brush, some in tents, and others on the cold ground with no covering but their blankets. By passing once through the grounds, we could find men suffering from all kinds of wounds. Here on a rough table the surgeons were amputating a leg, on another one's arm was being taken off, while a score of others just taken from the ambulances were awaiting their turn, with all manner of wounds claiming attention. There one could see what ever was. In the hospital after the wounds are dressed it is bad enough, but it is no comparison to the battle-field hospital. I saw one poor fellow belonging to a Texas Reg[iment] who had his leg almost torn off by a cannon ball just above the knee, the bones crushed and torn out, only adhereing to the trunk by a few pieces of skin, who had been bounced for nearly 6 miles in an old wagon of an ambulance over roads far from being good. Yet he was still alive and perfectly reliable in his speech.[10]

In moving the wounded, it was really heart rendering to listen to their groans and cries. Several had been shot directly through the bowels, and the least movement caused them to suffer intensely. After loading three trains with the wounded, we were called upon to bury three men who had died since being brought to the hospitals. We dug a shallow grave some three feet deep by 4 feet wide and laid the three poor soldiers in it side by side and covering them with their blankets. We covered them up as hastily as possible for day was fast approaching, and the enemies guns at Resaca, the light of burning bridges, and the reports of soldiers all told us that the enemy would soon be upon us. What a burial! Unknown, they were inhumanly, *treacherously,* buried by stranger hands. Yet, no doubt that they had fast and loving friends and relatives, who if they could, would have closed their eyes and performed the last sad rites of the dead, with tears in their eyes and sighs of true grief. But now their friends will never know where they sleep "the last unwaking sleep," for no rough board even marks their resting place. There is something terrible to me in this nameless resting place,—this unknown burial, I trust it may never be my lot to die and be burried thus.[11]

But let me hasten on. After burying the soldiers, we started down the Rail-Road to Calhoun. It was a weary some march, as we were very tired with our marching yesterday and our work all night. Calhoun is 22 miles South of Dalton on the R[ail] R[oad] and was undoubtedly a very pleasant place in peaceable times. The country now began to improve wonderfully. Fine rolling fields of wheat and grass, excellent farm-houses, showing wealth, refinement and taste in greater degree than any I have yet seen in this state. A mile or two below Calhoun we stoped to rest and sleep. Slept for two or three hours, then pursued our army again, the country improving as we went. Stopping to rest for one hour or so just after twelve, we had two days rations issued to us, consisting of hard bread and bacon. Within a mile of Adairsville, we camped for the night in a pleasant little grove near some good water, where no soldiers had camped before us. It was a lovely night, clear and pleasant, with a high moon shining from an unclouded sky. I lay down in my blanket and lighting my pipe, smoked and meditated for a long time, ere I felt like invoking the aid of Morpheus to dispel my weariness. What thoughts—sad, gloomy—yet why let one's thoughts wander there. We must take things as they come and be thankful that we live from day to day.[12]

We will have a busy day to-morrow, so I will write no more. Thus ends my days record, a sad one, yet I fear only one of many.

## Tuesday, May 17th

We were roused up last night about 12 o'clock by the Captain with orders to get ready to march immediately. It was hard, nevertheless I got up and put on my harness, then we commenced our weary road. Reaching the town of Adairsville, we took the Rail-Road and after a march of five miles, we camped until daylight in a very pleasant place near a lovely spring.[13]

The forenoon was passed in resting, most of the time in looking for our Division. About noon it rained very hard for an hour or two, after which we marched all the way back to town in the mud. Fixed a bridge or two, then marched back again.

This countermarching always provokes me, and to-day's work has put me in a very bad humour. Our army is still "falling

back" or retreating in slow and very good order. "Falling back"
is the army phrase when we don't want to acknowledge that he
is retreating. I think we will go back several days yet, perhaps all
the way to Atlanta.

[Major General John Bell] Hood's Corps, in which is our
Division, goes to Cassville from Adairsville, and we have to go
across to that road to-morrow morning early, so I will settle
myself for the night as soon as possible and try to make up for
lost sleep.14

A few clouds still stretch their shadows across the sky through
which the moon shines dimly.

———————————— *Wednesday, May 18th* ————————————

Up again at 2 o'clock this morning. "Attention!" "Fall in!"
Horrible sound, but Mr. *Military Power* says we must obey. So I
meekly arise, shake off the heavy God of slumber, fold up my
blanket, put on my knapsack and two haversacks and am ready
for duty.

Two miles east of this there is a road running to the town of
Cassville, county seat of Cass County. Nobody knew the road,
but several pretended to know it. Up a long narrow lane half-a-
mile, then—where then. Ah, "that's the question." The Captain
rides off to inquire. Soon returns with all the needful information, so he says. Off again. Over a rough stumpy road! Across
nearby creeks, where one gets his feet wet in getting over despite
his utmost care. Up to the corner of a field. No road to be traced
any farther. What then? Stop until daylight is the order, so that
we can *see* how to get out. So we stop just about one mile from
where we started, until day appears. How much more pleasant it
would have been to have slept until then in the first place, when
we could have traveled with ease and some little comfort. But
no, the power that is, thinks differently and he has a *will* if not a
*way* of his own. The friendly roof of an old deserted house
afforded us shelter from the damp, heavy dew.

Daylight appeared and we were off again. Through deep old forests, over fields of young corn, along rough hilly lanes, we marched until we reached the road we were in search of, when we found that we had just struck the head of our Division,—just in time.15

The country was very fine over which we traveled. Large plantations well tilled, great fields of wheat just heading out, all or nearly all to be destroyed by the army. Artillery men will pull down the fence wherever they happen to stop, and let their horses eat the wheat. Cavalry and staff officers ditto.16

It is horrible to see the havoc that a retreating army makes along its line of march. In this respect there is no difference as far as I can see, between friend and foe.17

Coming in sight of Cassville, we turned off to the west and camped in a lovely grove of young oaks and chesnuts. Cassville is situated in a lovely valley, surrounded by a rich agricultural country, and in times of Peace must have been a very pleasant place to live in. At all events, if the citizens here did not live well, it must have been their own fault, for it is a great country for small grain and fruit of all kinds. Peaches, above all the other fruit I think, thrives well here by the looks of the trees.18

_____ *Thursday May 19th* _____

We slept all night and late this morning without being disturbed. Glorious rest too. Ah, how I enjoyed it.

About ten o'cl[oc]k, we made a start. Firing in our front told that the enemy were still close after us. Falling back through town we took up our position on a range of hills running N E x S W. We were marched here and there for three or four hours up hills and down in ravines, cutting underbrush away from before our line of battle, and every thing else just to keep us busy. It does seem at times as though our Captain tried to see how much he could get for us to do, and he seems to have an idea that no one of us can ever get worn out. About five o'cl[oc]k, our line of battle was changed to another range of hills a half-mile farther back, where it is said the decisive battle is to be fought. After the line was formed, we were ordered to cut a road for the ambulances from the rear of our Division to the main road three quarters of a mile away. As my feet were very sore, I carried the baggage of some of the other boys. Soon the enemy got their guns in position and commenced throwing shells at our line. *Whizz-ing-hum,* they came bursting directly over our heads until the fire became too hot for us, When the order was given to get out of there as soon as possible. And such a "skedaddle"— "every body for himself and the devil take the hind most" was practically illustrated. Away the boys went through the woods and across the fields, until a place was reached beyond the range of the shells.[19] If the old gentleman in Black, called by tongues polite, "His Satanic Majesty," had really taken the hindmost, I would have gone up sure. As my pedal extremities would not admit of fast traveling and as I was overloaded with baggage, I had to walk along the best way I could while all the balance ran. My first impulse was to throw down the knapsacks and blankets with which I was encumbered, and I thought the owners might have relieved me of them, but a second thought caused me to push ahead. The shells bursting directly over me, and the pieces flew about my head, cutting the branches right and left. At least I got out of range and was soon relieved of my extra amount of traps. Halting in an old field, we waited for night to close in so that the firing would cease when we could go back and finish our work without danger.[20]

Our rations were out to-day and our commisary left us this morning for a fresh supply, but has not returned. I ate a good breakfast this morning, for dinner I ate a couple of crackers and a little raw ham. As I had two large crackers left, I called up one of messmates who had nothing since morning and divided with him. I cannot bear to see any of my friends with nothing to eat as long as I have any, and I will divide, although No. 1 is the rule here in the army. I doubt if any of the company would divide with me if I was out and they had anythng. "Take care of No. 1." That is it.

Finished cutting our road through the woods, then got ready about ten o'clock to start for the Division hospitals about two miles off, towards Cassville. It was a clear, lovely moonlight night and the road was crowded with wagons, artillery, men, horses, anything that constitutes an army. There is every prospect of a terrible battle to-morrow.[21]

Gen[eral Joseph E.] Johnston has issued an order telling the soldiers that he has fallen back "far enough and now the day has to be decided by a great battle."[22] Heaven help the poor careless wretches, who see the moon, shining upon this sinful world for the last time.

Heavy skirmishing for a mile or more along our line occupied half an hour or more just before dark in which we lost several prisoners. Our Captain selected a miserable place to camp. On a hill where we had to work half an hour or so to get the rocks out, so as to lay down with anything like comfort. Lighting my pipe, I lay down to rest. Tobacco is a great solace to the soldier. It relieves one's mind more than aught else.

_____ *Friday May 20th* _____

The army is a poor place for me who professes to be a good prophet. Everything last night betokened a desperate fight to-day, in fact Gen'l Johnston so stated in his orders of yesterday morning. Yet last night, or rather this morning about three o'cl[oc]k, we received orders to get up and march. So away we went, and such marching. It was a sort of dog trot all the way. There was more hurry and confusion than anything I have yet seen in this retreat. Cannoniers [and] wagon[eer]s whipping their horses, officers yelling to their respective commands to "close up," and everybody and everything serving to do their best to get ahead.[23]

We reached Cartersville, a pleasant, business little town, on the R[ail] R[oad] just one [and] a half miles north of the Etowah river just as day was breaking. Resting here an hour, we went on and crossed the river on a splendid bridge some 15 feet above the water.[24] As I had no breakfast, I concluded to set some cornmeal if I could and cook me some breakfast as soon as we stoped. Some cook wagons near the railroad caused me to go there and ask for some corn-meal. Didn't have any. A second attempt ended in the same way, and I made no more. It was the first time I had ever asked for anything to eat, and it will be the last. As sacks upon sacks of corn meal are thrown away on every retreat, I was not prepared for a refusal, but it is all right I suppose. The last man I asked refused me very shortly although I told him I would pay him a dollar a quart for it, whereupon I replied in these words, "Very well, sir. Whenever you get out of rations to eat for a day or two just call on me [and] I will divide my last cracker with you."[25]

I did not care about it for myself, so much as I did for some of the boys who have had nothing to eat since yesterday morning, besides there is no prospect of getting anything to-day. After marching round for an hour or two, we finally located on a stretch of hillside covered with rocks, overlooking the broad level bottom of the river. It is a miserable place seeing we have the selection of our own camp, and in fair range of the enemies guns from the hills on the opposite side of the river. I expected, as it is the general impression we will stay here all day, that the Captain would send some one to hunt up our Comissary, for we have moved so much since he left that it would be a hard matter for him to find us—but nothing of the kind. He seemed to be perfectly content as he had enough to eat, and the suffering of his men did not trouble him at all. I know that if I had been Captain of this Company, I would have had rations for them to-day sure. This is the second time in my life that I have really suffered for something to eat. Once before out on the plains.[26]

Night has come [and] I will forget my hunger in sleep.

—————————— *Saturday, May 21st* ——————————

We were up and off by daylight this morning. After traveling about a mile we overtook a wagon loaded with crackers that had broken down on the road, and you ought to have seen us impress them. I got enough for two meals at least, and then we went on about a mile farther, when we camped again, as they say for a day or two. Soon had a fire built and frying some meat. I soon had a nice mess of stewed or fried crackers, off of which I made a hearty meal and now feel in a pretty good humour again. We are camped in a lovely place by the side of a clear stream of running water, very good and sweet.[27]

Took a general wash. Put on some clean clothes and now feel like a new man. Wrote to [J. J.] Aughe and Miss Mary J[ane] W[alker]. Our rations came in this morning, biscuit for two days, and such biscuit! I intend to save one for a curiosity. The flour was mixed with water and then baked, making a ball of black, hard substance—a very poor substitute for cannon balls should we ever get out of those instruments of death. Corn bread for two days—two pones to the man. Hardly enough for one day, and bacon for four days—plenty of that at all events. So we had a dinner, if not extra good in quality, was at least extra in quantity. Ate too much as I have a dull headache, caused I think by the soggy black biscuit.[28]

—————————— *Sunday May 22d.* ——————————

> Oh blessed day of rest,
> The holiest and the best
> Of all the seven
> From which our heart doth yearn
> That we may therein learn
> The way to Heaven.

It has indeed been a day of rest to me, and if ever a man enjoyed it, I am sure that I did. How it was passed, I scarcely know,—in a kind of dreamy trance, half-awake, half-asleep,—at all events, I rested gloriously.

Wrote to "Ma," also to F. M. B[radley] so that I am now even with my correspondents once more. That is some consolation at all events. Also received a letter from F. M. B[radley] this evening.

Directly after dinner, I went over to the 24th Ala[bama] Reg[imen]t to see Geo[rge] Caulfield, and I passed an hour very pleasantly talking over Theatricals with George who was a member of the same company I was in in Mobile. Also saw some more of the Mobile boys, and had a pleasant time recalling the reminences of other days. Returning to camp, I rested gloriously the balance of the day. Towards night orders came to get ready to leave at a moment's warning, so packed up all my things then lay down to get all the rest I could. As our orders came before 10 o'c[loc]k we went to bed in spread out blankets and went to sleep, but as I was expecting we would leave at any hour, I could not rest very well.[29]

_____ *Monday May 23d.* _____

All the forenoon we lay under the shade of our beeches and was thankful to the powers that be for such a long respite from our expected duties. Directly after dinner we were ordered to repair the roads to Allatoona. So climbing over the mountains to the east, we commenced our labors. And such a road! A good sized stream—it might be termed a river, wound its serpentine course round among mountains and hills, rushing and foaming over great rocks that sometimes formed small caskades. The steep banks on either side running entirely down to the waters edge. On one side of this stream, the road ran, scooped out of the bank sometimes fifty feet above the river. The road was in a bad condition and it required a good deal of work. So that night we found we had proceeded over 1½ miles. Camped at a mill and iron furnace on the river where some deserted house furnished us with a roof to keep the heavy dew off, but the floor I noticed was much harder than the ground, consequently I did not sleep very soundly.[30]

I obtained some fresh corn meal at the mill and mixing up some batter, I baked me some nice cakes for supper. Perhaps it was eating too much of those articles that caused me a bad night rest. The clouds last night betokened rain but beyond a light sprinkle they passed away. It is the poorest country here I have ever seen. Even the streams have no bottom land [and] there are no vallies between the hills, all ravines, not an acre of tillable land.[31]

_____ *Tuesday May 24th* _____

After repairing the road some miles below the mill this morning, we struck a better portion of the country where the roads were in good repair, consequently we shouldered our knapsacks and started for Allatoona. It is simply a R[ail] R[oad] station and depot for iron found in the mountains near by. The dust was very thick so that we determined to keep ahead of the division. Down the rail-road two miles there off to the west on the Lost M[ountain] road. The enemy it seems have flanked us again and we are now on a race to get a position ahead of them. After proceeding some three miles we found that we were on the wrong road, so we had to go back a mile and a half and repair the road over some streams to get Artillery over.[32] It was a hard job and did not improve any tempers much, which was at best not in a very good mood. After finishing our work we got ahead of the Division again and was head on until the middle of the afternoon, or say 4 o'cl[oc]k, when we camped in a thick woods of young trees.

Soon had a fire built, and baked me some batter cakes, so that I ate a hearty supper, then lay down to rest for I was very weary. Soon the dark clouds in the west, and the low peals of thunder, warned in that we might prepare for a storm. Erected our tent and put our things under. It commenced raining about dusk, and a hard rain it was for nearly half the night, but as we were safe from it, we slept well, all but Billy McMullen who had a severe chill about midnight.[33]

——————————— *Wednesday May 25th* ———————————

I make this record with the musketry and cannon roaring along our line of battle. We were up and off early this morning over a rough and rugged road for some eight or ten miles when we reached New Hope Church, situated on a high ridge running like all ridges and mountains in Georgia that I have seen, N E [and] S W. We had scarcely gained our position before our pickets and those of the enemy met and commenced firing. We were just in time to secure our position. The Division was immediately wheeled in line of battle and our company was ordered to the hospitals in the rear. Soon after reaching there the wounded began to pour in. It seems that the 58th [and] 32d Ala[bama] Reg[iments] consolidated, were out on picket, and in advancing came suddenly upon the enemy drawn up in line of battle, who received them with a volley that killed and wounded some thirty odd men. It must have been a most miserably managed affair.[34]

After the Surgeons had selected a suitable place for their hospitals, we had to go to work and build arbors for the wounded. About an hour and a half before dark the engagement became general along our lines, and I heard the heaviest firing I ever listened to. The vollies of small arms were continuous, so that we could not distinguish the single report of a musket, while the cannonading was terrific. Soon the ambulances of the different Brigades began to come in, loaded with wounded. You can see all kinds of wounds, slight [and] mortal.[35]

——————————— *Thursday May 26th* ———————————

Another day of battle, and no material advantage gained on either side as far as I can learn. The firing between the pickets was kept up all night long, so as to keep the men on either side from working on their breastworks. My Regiment, however, managed to get very fair works erected so that they have not suffered much as yet.[36] We were up [and] at work this morning early, after a very poor night's rest. It rained the greater part of the night and as we had no time to put up our tent until after it commenced, we fared rather badly. Just before 12 o'cl[oc]k we were ordered to the front to cut out some rock, not a very desirable job when a battle is raging. We cut it out, however, in short order and, as most of it was in a ravine, the balls passed harmlessly over our heads. Finished it about three o'clock, when we returned to our quarters and after a hearty meal, lay down to rest. The firing to-day has not been very heavy nor continuous, yet the wounded pour in very fast. The enemy do not seem to care about attacking us in force, but I think are maneuvering to flank us again.[37] If so, the decisive battle will not be fought here. After burying a few of our dead, we selected a good camping place, and beneath the thick leaved branches of a chestnut, I propose to pass the night. It has been a very pleasant day. Cool and comfortable. Very cool this evening so that a fire is not out of place.

_____ *Friday May 27th* _____

And still another day of wholesale murder and nothing done to decide the day. After a good night's rest, we were up and at work early this morning, putting up additional arbors and bury-ing the dead. You—I mean the "gentle reader"—If ever any eye but my own should take the trouble to read these pages, and supposing that "gentle reader" has never been through the "glorious pomp and circumstance of war" in all its horrid reality—you have never seen a soldier shot on the battle field, burried—well let me devote a few lines to the subject. The soldier is mortally wounded on the field, but not quite dead. He is borne on a litter to a safe position where the ambulances of his Brigade takes him to the Hospital. There the Doctor perhaps pronounces his case hopeless, and he is laid aside where he lingers for an hour, perhaps a day, then dies. If there is any hope his wound is dressed, then perhaps he dies after a day or so, and he meets soldier's burial, in the same clothes in which he died, unwashed, smeared in his gore—a horrid sight. We dig him a grave, two feet deep, wrap him in his blanket, if he has one, and cover him up. Such is a soldiers burial at the hospital.[38]

About ten o'cl[oc]k, we received orders to report to Gen[eral Alexander Peter] Stewart. Upon reporting to him we were ordered to report to Gen[eral Alpheus] Baker for work on his breastworks.[39] Horrid to work on breastworks during an engagement, with the enemies lines within 150 yards of ours. The firing, however, was too hot for us to do anything and so we were ordered to hold ourselves in readiness by the time the firing ceased, or nearly so when we could do the work. We were about one hundred yards behind our reserve line of battle and the balls flew in every direction around us. We were in a more exposed place in fact than those behind the breastworks. Nearly all the boys got down behind trees. I lay down behind a small tree but as we were exposed to an enfilading fire it did not protect me much. First a ball would whiz over me to the right, then another would come from the left. Soon their cannon opened and the grape and canister fell like hail around us.[40]

I do not claim to be blessed with any extra amount of bravery, but at all events, I can safely say I did not exhibit quite as much cowardice as some in the company. As every ball whistled by, some three or four would dodge behind the nearest tree, and when the grape and canister shot began to fall around us, they sought logs and crept down behind them like a parcel of startled partridges, seeking the friendly protection of a hedge. Two or three of them suddenly disappeared when the cannon opened, and were seen no more until we move half way back to camp. Yet one of these men says he was detailed as a wagon driver in the K[entucky] expedition under [General Edmund] Kirby Smith,[41] and at the battle of Richmond, he left his team to enter the fight. Bah! His movements today has proven his assertions to be false and he a braggart.

As the firing grew heavier, we returned to Camp to get something to eat about three o'clock with orders to return at dark and work all night on the breastworks. Fine prospect for a weary man, but it is one of the stern necessities of war.

On reaching camp, I soon had dinner prepared and ate hearty. We then had to burry some more dead soldiers, a job by no means pleasant, yet one that we soon get hardened to, like everything else. I then lay down and tried to rest a little as there is no prospect of any to-night. The artillery fire of the enemy is very heavy and our wounded are coming in by the scores.[42]

---

## Saturday May 28th

After one of the most wearisome days of the campaign, I sit down to-night to make a brief record. We got to work on the breastworks last night about 9 o'cl[oc]k in front of the 37th Ala[bama] Reg[iment], who lost some seventy odd men in an hour or more by the enemy's artillery fire. It is not very pleasant working on breastworks all night, when the sharpshooters or pickets of both sides are banging away every few moments to keep either side from fortifying. Whiz-iz the balls would fly just over our heads, sometimes in rather close proximity. About three o'cl[oc]k in the morning, when the moon had got fairly up, the enemy made an assault upon our lines to the right of us and the musketry roared incessantly for some time.[43] The R[egiment] on whose breastworks we were working, fell out. On reporting to Gen[eral A. P.] Stewart, we were ordered to go to camp for our baggage and report back immediately. The hospitals were fully two miles off and it was a weary walk, tired as we were. We returned just at daybreak and soon the whole Division was in motion.[44]

Then commenced one of the strangest movements of the whole campaign. Along the crookedest roads to be found, across streams, up hills, down in ravines, we pursued our weary way until finally we passed within twenty-five yards of our camp. That was somewhat provoking, but on we went towards the Rail Road, in an easterly direction. About noon we turned to the north, then to the west, and about an hour by [the] sun, we arrived at the very spot we crossed the road at in the morning. Our movements constituted a figure 8—thus $\frac{1}{2}\!\mathcal{8}$ —the figure 1 representing the starting point, and the figure 2 where we are to-day camped. I judge we have traveled some 18 miles to-day. I presume this strange movement can be accounted for by the supposition that the enemy were trying to flank us on our right, and our Division was ordered there to repel this, but ere we reached the designated spot, the supposition was found to be erroneous. Consequently we were marched back by a different route. I am very weary.

—————————— *Sunday May 29th* ——————————

A lovely Sabbath day. I would much rather hear the church bells ringing forth their solemn yet pleasant invitations for us to pass the day like christians and civilized people than for the engines of war to proclaim in their thunder notes that we pass it amid scenes of carnage and death, like barbarians.

About eight o'cl[oc]k we were off to the right again. After an hour's march we were halted to rest for a while near a farm house where a fine apple orchard afforded some very pleasant shade. Fortunately our rest continued for about two hours. At the end of that time, we marched on a mile or two farther, where our Division was formed in line of battle.[45]

Our first duty was to cut out woods, first for our ambulances, then for Artillery. It was a tiresome job, and I felt much more weary than I did last night. We worked on our Artillery road, until about ten o'clock when we lay down to rest. There has been no general engagement at this end of the lines to-day, the firing being confined to skirmishes on both sides. The casualties have been very slight, in fact I have only heard of one man in our Division being wounded. We were exposed to the fire all the afternoon, but generally the balls passed harmlessly over our heads.[46]

When will this long struggle be decided? It cannot be delayed much longer it seems to me.

—————————— *Monday May 30th* ——————————

We were at work by daylight this morning on our Artillery road. Finished in about two hours, then returned to our camp. Ate a hearty breakfast. Soon after Gen[eral Alexander Peter] Stewart treated us to a good drink of whiskey and told us we could rest for awhile as he had nothing for us to do just then. A very agreeable order! Lay down and slept until noon, when I prepared and ate dinner. Then wrote a letter to Miss Mary J[ane] W[alker] and sent it off to be mailed. Soon after I received a letter from her—a sad one too, wherein she stated that she had lost a very dear friend a few days before, by a pistol shot in a quarrel, and, she morned his loss in a manner that caused me to feel far from pleasant memories, as I am by Death who is each day reaping such an abundant harvest.

We have rested all day, and it has been very quiet all along the lines. Some new movements will be developed ere long I think.

When I see the effects of war on every side of me, I think of and respect Bulwer's lines in "Richelieu."

> "Thou dark and fallen *Angel,* whose name on Earth's
> *Ambition*—thou make it thy throne on treasures,
> stratagems, and murder, and with thy fierce and bloodest
> smile canst quench the grinding stars of Heaven's empire—
> hear us, for we are thine—and light us to the goal!"[47]

The weather is very fine, clear and warm—with cool nights. I do not feel well to-night.

_____ *Tuesday May 31st* _____

Rested until near night when we received orders to report for duty at the Division's Hospitals. Reached there just at sundown.

_____ *Wednesday* _____

Worked the greater part of the day on a coffin for Major [Winfrey B.] Scott of the 19th L[ouisiana] Reg[iment]. Returned to our old camp at night and worked on an artillery road 'till dark.[48]

_____ *Thursday* _____

Rested most of the day. It commenced raining about noon and had several heavy showers during the P.M.

_____ *Friday* _____

Was cloudy and rained almost all day. Twenty of the Co[mpany] went to Lost M[ountain], 6 miles below here to cut out roads.[49]

_____ *Sat[urday]* _____

Rained all night nearly, and until about ten o'cl[oc]k this morning. At 12 left for a new camp half a mile below. About an hour by sun, the wagons and troops began to move south. Another "fall back."[50] Got ready what food there was left started. It commenced to rain about the same time, which added to the uncomfortableness of our marching. The roads too were almost impossible on account of the mud. We went some two miles, when myself and a companion were left to build a signal fire. The rain was pouring down and we found it rather a difficult matter to get a fire started. At last we succeeded, when we built a rude shelter which protected us from the rain in a measure. It was a most horrible night for traveling and the roads were lined with wagons getting stalled in the mud every few minutes.

_____ *Sunday 5th June* _____

Again it is the Holy Sabbath day, but mercy what a day! We were up and off by four o'cl[oc]k this morning. It was so dark that we could not see which way to go, while the mud was half-knee deep. The road was lined with soldiers trying to march, and every movement would witness the *fall* of several brave fellows, but up they would get and travel on again. It was a horrid morning, such as I hope never to see again, under such circumstances. I was bedaubed with mud up to my waist, for in places it was a perfect lob-lolly, then again it was stiff and dry, so that we could hardly walk through it. About ten o'cl[oc]k we reached Lost M[ountain] where we came up with the balance of the Company. Some two or three miles farther we wended our weary way, the roads getting higher, but fortunately not so muddy, until we came to a halt on a ridge running due N[orth and South] some two miles East of Lost M[ountain]. The troops were here formed in line of battle, and we rested the balance of the day. I never felt so weary. My legs ached so that I could not sleep, and then my head ached painfully. Must put a stop to it, else I shall suffer by it.[51]

It cleared off about noon and having a slight shower, the sun shone with intense heat the rest of the day. We are now within 8 miles of Marietta. Whether a battle will be fought here or not, I have no idea. I hardly think there will though. Yet I may be mistaken, as wiser men often are.[52]

_____ *Monday June 6th* _____

As I wish to post the result of this Campaign in this volume, I shall only note the days as briefly as possible. Was on the sick list today. No fighting in our new positions yet.

——————————————— *Tuesday. 7th* ———————————————

Still on the sick list, and feel rather badly. Hope the medicine I took this morning however will have the desired effect.

——————————————— *Wed[nesday] 8th* ———————————————

Received marching orders after an early breakfast. Went some five or six miles and camped S[outh] W[est] of the Kenesaw M[ountain]. Rained at night.

——————————————— *Thurs[day] 9th* ———————————————

Cut out roads on line of battle nearly all day. Moved at night up on R[ail] R[oad]. Showerery [*sic*] again.

——————————————— *Fri[day] 10th* ———————————————

Rained nearly all night.

——————————————— *Sat[urday] 11th* ———————————————

Moved up on the right again this morning in the midst of a heavy rain. Cut out roads.

——————————————— *Sun[day] 12th* ———————————————

Rained very hard all night nearly and most of the day.

——————————————— *Mon[day] 13th* ———————————————

Rained all night again, and all the forenoon. Cool this evening.

——————————————— *Tues[day] 14th* ———————————————

Clear and cool this morning. Gen[eral Leonidas] Polk was killed about noon to-day by a cannon shot. Rested all day.[53]

──────────────── *Wed[nesday] 15th* ────────────────

Clear still [and] pleasant. Cannonading along the lines commenced early this morning. One half of my Reg[iment], 40th Ala[bama] was captured while out on picket to-day.[54]

──────────────── *Thurs[day] 16th* ────────────────

Were ordered to follow the Division which had gone to the right again. Were busy all day cutting roads.

──────────────── *Friday 17th* ────────────────

This morning after breakfast, I anticipated a good days rest and consequently got out my writing materials and sat down at the root of a tree to write some letters. Was just in the middle of my epistle when I was interrupted by a courier from Gen[eral] John Bell] Hood with orders to report to Gen[eral] H[ood]'s headquarters.

Then commenced a long very rigorous march of several miles. The duty we had to perform was to cut out a line of battle on Kenesaw M[ountain]. It took us all day nearly. On reaching the top a grand view was obtained. The country was spread out in panoramic view beneath us, and we could see for miles on every side. At a station on the R[ail] R[oad] called Big Shanty hundreds—I do not know but I might say thousands of Yankee wagons could be seen, while nearby we could distinguish their lines of battle opposite ours. A few of their guns were firing and some 15 were plainly seen firing on our lines.[55]

──────────────── *Sat[urday] June 18th* ────────────────

I did intend to preserve a few pages to note the result of this campaign, but as it seems a good ways off, I will note a few days proceeding and close the volume. We left Kenesaw M[ountain] and returned to Gen[eral] Stewart's H[ea]d Q[uarter]s last night. It looked something like rain, so we spread our little tent and lay down to sleep. About four o'cl[oc]k this morning, I was awakened by the rain, and in a short time it settled down in a steady heavy rain that continued until about 11 o'clock. I lay under the tent until it ceased, or rather slacked up before I ventured out to get breakfast. Then ate and attempted to dry my shawl. The Captain went up to headquarters to see what orders there were for us, [and] soon returned with the intelligence that the house was deserted. Learned that our Division had moved down to the left to reinforce the line there.56 Then the march commenced that will long be remembered. The rain had rendered the roads almost impassable to footmen and to wagons too. Putting on my things and spreading my part of our tent over my shoulders, we started off. Just at this time it commenced raining again.57

Through the mud and mire we purused our way until we reached Kenesaw M[ountain]. Here, as the roads were higher, they were not quite so muddy. After four hour's marching we reached our Division, where we put in to making bridges for the infantry across the streams, swollen to an almost impassable height by the heavy rains. Just at dusk the Division was ordered back again. My pen can never do justice to the night's march. By some misstep I soon got over my shoes in mud, then getting careless, I no more attempted to pick my way, but splashing in through thick and thin, I hurried on. Our road lay on the South side of Kenesaw, over a very rough road. Coming to a stream, dashing down the mountain side, we would plunge in, regardless of the depth of water, then wade through mud half knee deep. All our lines are falling back. Kenesaw M[ountain] being the Centre, then the right and left wings extending nearly due east and west.58

Reaching the Marietta road, we followed it for a mile or so until we got in the suburbs of the village, then we were ordered to countermarch, back nearly the whole mile, and away off to the right again. It was just ½ past 12 o'cl[oc]k, when a halt was ordered and we were told to camp. And such a camp. Wet and covered with mud, the ground cold and wet,—but pshaw! nothing to a soldier. We soon had a roaring fire, and laying some rails on the ground, I lay down [and] was soon sound asleep.[59]

—————————— *Sunday June 19th/64* ——————————

The last record I shall make in this volume, and anything but pleasant has the events been to me.

I was roused up this morning about eight o'cl[oc]k by the order to fall in for duty. It was still raining and had been nearly all night. So wrapping up my wet blankets, I reported ready. After walking about two miles in the rain and mud, we found our line of battle, and proceeded to cut it out, one-hundred yards wide. About noon, after a couple of hours sun shine, it clouded up again and such a rain as we had for about an hour I have seldom witnessed. It poured down, and reminded me of the saying of an old friend of mine—"not only were the windows of Heaven opened, but the sash all knocked out and doors took off the hinges."[60]

After it was over, we again commenced work, and continued it until about 6 o'cl[oc]k when we were ordered back to the Division as it was again going down on the left, or rather to the Centre.

Oh, horrible! Most horrible! There was no use in picking one's way. You might as well *wade* in at once. So in I went. You could find mud and water at all depths, and every consistency of thickness from two or three up to ten and twelve inches. Fortunately we had daylight to get over the worst part of our roads, and we reached our destination just at dark.

The shells and solid shot from the enemies batteries flew over our heads as we were passing the mountain base, but I believe they done no damage, only scaring some of our boys pretty badly.[61] When we reached our camping place, we were fortunate enough to find the loft of a corn-crib, or some other outhouse in which to sleep. Building up a fire, I soon had supper cooked and ate hearty as I had eaten nothing since nine o'cl[oc]k this morning. The supper was only a duplicate of every meal nearly that I have eaten since this campaign commenced— namely bacon fried and cold corn bread cut in slices fried in the grease. Of course I am very tired of such fare, nevertheless it goes pretty well when one has a good appetite and is really hungry as I was.

My record is about ended as far as this volume goes. I intend however to continue it in another volume, and if I live to finish it, it will present a history, as far as I am concerned, of one of the most tedious, and at the same time active, campaigns on record. I hope in the next to chronicle the end of the campaign and also this unholy and bloody war. Let every heart respond "Amen."

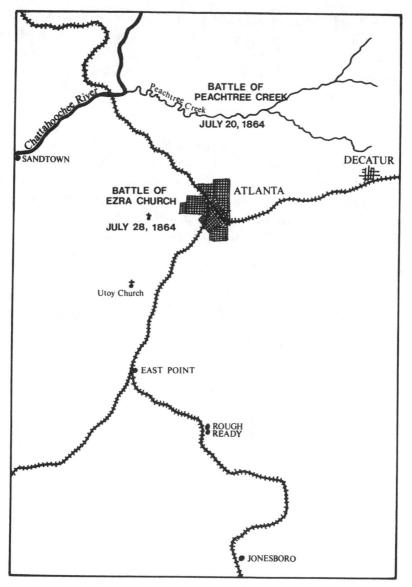

MAP 3.
The Battle of Atlanta
JUNE–SEPTEMBER 1864

# 4

# Atlanta

## Camp-Life

The morning of the 21st day of June dawned upon us with clouds and rain. It was very disagreeable and unpleasant for us to remain in camp even. How much more so to march several long, dreary miles. The order to get breakfast and pack up for marching dispelled all pleasing anticipation of a day of rest, so we started a fire as well as we could and fried a little meat which we ate with our cold corn bread, although it seemed like a mockery of the good old times, to say that we had *breakfasted.* "Fall In!" Oh certainly, hurry up—yes, yes,—on with your things, and away we go to march in [the] distant—some mile and-a-half, over a very rough and muddy road. What a day! The long continued rains had rendered the roads almost impassable, and then the rain, not a dashing, spirited shower, but a slow, steady, drizzling rain, as though the vapor that hung mid-way between heaven and Earth was halting between two opinions, and had not yet decided whether to remain above or fall down upon the blood stained mess, which we call "Our World."

Marietta, as war put its desolating hands upon it, was a lovely inland town—five business houses, and elegant suburban residences, but Alas! Now it looks anything but romantic and beautiful. The business houses turned into hospitals or depots for army stores, and the residences abandoned by their wealthy owners, all going to ruin beneath the soldier's wanton touch.[1]

We passed through the village hurriedly and took the Powder Springs road. A march of four miles to the S[outh] W[est], then a half in the rain waiting for orders from the powers that be. Then our bagges goes in a corn crib for security and shelter, while we go to work on roads. We had cut a road half a mile or more through a thick wood, then the order is given to work on some other road, and lastly that order is terminated and we go to work on a bridge across a deep rapid stream, swollen by the recent rains to an overflowing state—how provoking! In the water and now up to my knees, cutting stringers thirty-five feet long, then carrying and placing them in their proper places. I do assure you it was far from sport.[2]

As I have said, we ate breakfast early this morning and after our march of 6 miles, then to march on until dark, with nothing more to eat, was far from pleasant, yet we done it, and when night came, wet, muddy, tired and in a very bad humor, we returned to camp, a mile distant, to cook our humble repast, and eat it, or else go supperless to bed. Near where we were at work was an orchard, and I got a lot of June apples, nearly ripe, which I stewed for supper. Add to this I met some St. Louis boys, who gave me a cup of good strong coffee, so that I made a good healthy supper, after which I dried myself by a roaring fire, and about ten o'clock went to bed in a large gin house, half filled with cotton, making a soft comfortable bed, so that I slept very well. Thus ended a very disagreeable day in the "Georgia Campaign."

—————————————— *Wednesday 22nd* ——————————————

Up and off to work on our bridge before day light this morning, for they are in a great hurry for it, that is the engineers say they are. Although I doubt if a single [man] goes across it after it is finished. By nine o'clock we had it finished, and had corduroyed the swamp 150 yards wide, and the job was pronounced finished. Returning to camp we breakfasted, after which we rested. The rain had ceased, and the sun shone out very warm and pleasant. Going out in the apple orchard before spoken of, I got some half-bushel of apples and a beef's liver. The orchard by the "surly river" in front of our lines, and comprised some fifty acres of wheat as fine a field I have seen and just about ripe enough for the sickle, all to be destroyed. Oh, but it is sickening to see such destruction. Our Division came down to-day. I saw Lt. [James W.] M[onett], who gave me a package from Mobile in which I found a box of sardines and half-a-dozen fine cigars.[3]

For supper I had apples, beef liver, bacon and corn bread. A very fine supper by the way, to which I did ample justice. After it, I smoked a cigar and thought of old times, a very pleasing occupation while it lasts. The fighting on the left commenced about three o'clock and has been very desperate all the rest of the P.M. I never saw so many wounded men before, they came out in gangs of ten, twenty and even more, besides the ambulances filled with those who were wounded too badly to walk. Poor fellows! All kinds and manners of wounds in the head, body, arms, legs. Oh, but it is sickening to look at them. We lay and watched them go by, thankful to think that we were out of it, but expecting every moment to be called on for duty. The order did not come, however, and we had the satisfaction to see the sun go down and hear the incessant roll of musketry and cannon cease. One more day of blood passed away.[4]

——————————— *Thursday 23rd* ———————————

Another day's work on our extreme left, cutting out a line of battle down as far as the Sandtown road, and without dinner, too, but very pleasant, but it is one of the evils we must submit too. It has been warm and pleasant, and as we drawed coffee, sugar [and] bacon to-night, we have managed to get ready for our nightly repose with our appetites appeased. So smoking another cigar, I set down with some of the boys and talked about the good old times we used to see when our meals were ready cooked for us, and when we could go where we pleased and return when we pleased.[5]

──────────── *Friday 24th June* ────────────

There is so much sameness about these days of duty. The same week over and over again that I find it impossible to narrate the events of each day so as to make it at all interesting, therefore, I will be very brief. Worked on roads all day the same as yesterday. At night camped at Gen[eral Alexander Peter] Stewart's H[ead] Q[uarters] in a thick grove of young wood.

──────────── *Saturday 25th* ────────────

Had nothing to do today, so we rested and had peas for dinner. Very warm, in fact, *hot*!

──────────── *Sunday 26th* ────────────

Rested until noon. Generally, as will be seen by one who takes the trouble to look over Vol[ume] I, Sunday is the busiest day of the week with us. Consequently, I thought it strange that we should rest, even until noon. We did however, then we were ordered to fall in and go down to the extreme left at the Sandtown Road to cut a line of battle still farther down.

Some mile or so we went until we reached the residence of an old gentleman by the name of Hamilton.[6] The line of battle was near his house, and, great god, what destruction, but it is the same story over again, fences pulled down, crops destroyed *et cetera*. The old gentleman was packing up and preparing to move to Mississippi. He had a son, a cripple, who had rather a novel contrivance for traveling over the county. He had a little wagon with three wheels, the front one fixed so as to guide the vehicle, and then he had a goat trained to push the wagon with

his head. It was very ingenuous, and very pleasant to travel over
the county. The cripple told me he had often gone twenty miles
per day over good roads. Here I came across a sweet little girl,
granddaughter of Mr. H[amilton], named Martha Ellen Smith.
What will be her fate, thus to be nurtured amid the stern and
horrid realities of war. So young, so beautiful [and] yet to pass
through such a fiery ordeal. We returned to camp before dark,
and passed a pleasant evening before retiring.

———————————— *Monday June 27th* ————————————

Very hot. I was awakened this morning by day-light or before
by a very heavy cannonading along our lines, extending to the
extreme right. A thousand-and-one rumors prevail as this has
been a heavy charge on the line occupied by [General Benjamin F.] Cheatham's Division. We hear that the enemy were cut
down by the thousand, but, hah!, we have heard too much of
that before this to believe it all. We know, or at least feel, that
we will have to leave this line, as well as all the rest that we have
occupied since we left Dalton, and [General William Tecumseh]
Sherman is going to do no more fighting than he is compelled to
do to keep up appearances.[7]

———————————— *Tuesday 28th* ————————————

We moved our camp South East a mile or so where we rested
the balance of the day by a lovely spring of the coldest water I
ever drank. *Wednesday* we went to where the Sandtown road
crosses our line and commenced putting up a fort on which we
worked all day. Very hot and very sultry. *Thursday:* I felt very
unwell, but still worked a little.

———————————— *Friday, July 1st* ————————————

Went up to the right of our division to lay off a fort like the
one to the left. Saturday worked as heretofore. Heavy cannonading this morning. When we returned to our camp we

received orders to get ready for to leave this position. So our hard work on the forts as usual is done for nought, as not a gun has been in them, much less fired out of them. About 10 o'cl[oc]k P.M. we left. A dark cloudy night, but the roads are getting good, so that we got along extremely well. After going some four miles, we stoped at a creek and built a large signal fire, where the troops could see how to cross the stream.[8] As the troops soon commenced passing, of course I could not sleep much for they made enough noise to wake the dead. One more move besides this and I think we will cross the Chattahoochee and then "Good bye" to Atlanta, for the thriving young city of Rail-Roads will go up, sooner or later sure.

──────────── *Monday July 4th 1864* ────────────

So this is the *glorious* "Fourth" I used to think about and dream about and talk about in my young days. Little did I dream however when I listened to the roar of cannon *then* that I would ever on that day hear the deep-mouthed monsters vomiting forth, not only fire and smoke, the harmless burning of gunpowder, but shot and shell in dead earnest. Yet it is ever so. Here on this warm summer July morning I can listen to the cannon's roar and hear the bursting of shell as I work away on a bridge across a stream up here in (I suppose) Cobb County, Georgia.

Yesterday we reached this position and soon after went to work on a redoubt which occupied us until dark. This morning, as before hinted, we went to work on an artillery bridge. For the past two or three days we have been on rather short rations and yesterday I managed to get some peas. One of my mess had to be excused because of sickness, so that he cooked them, and as I was determined to have my dinner, I left work and went up to camp in company with a mess-mate. We ate dinner and was returning when we met the cavalry coming in, who reported that the enemy had turned our left flank and were coming on rapidly. We hurried on down to the bridge and found our company all confusion as the enemy were in sight not over half-a-mile off, hurring on, and firing rapidly, while the balls fell thick and fast around us.[9]

The first thing I thought about was that I had eaten my dinner. We reached Camp in safety, and after resting a few minutes, we left for a new camp, but soon the enemy shelled us away still farther to the rear. It was by this time dark and resting on the side of a hill we silently awaited the arrival of our army, for of course, we had to fall back again.

Will this falling back never come to an end?

—————————— *Tuesday July 5th* ——————————

We left our position last night about two o'clock and marched until eight o'clock this morning. This brought us to within some two or three miles of the [Chattahoochee] river. After working an hour or two on roads, we reported to Gen[eral] Stewart's H[ea]d Quarters where we camped. We got a bountiful supply of Irish potatoes here, which we cooked for dinner and a good dinner we made of it. Such a dinner as I have long wanted in fact, and really I never knew how good Irish potatoes were before. We also found thousands of blackberries and we ate as many as we wanted of them.

About an hour by the sun we were ordered to fall in, and in a few minutes we were off for the river.[10] Before reaching it, we had a large corn-field to cross, some two miles I think, and in going across this field, so fast did our Captain ride that we lost sight of him entirely. Arriving at the pontoon bridge we naturally supposed he had crossed and over we went. It was very dark [and] the confusion and noise were almost equal to Babel. There was only two or three with me, but after going some half-a-mile South of the river, I found one of our Lieutenants and some dozen or more of the boys who had tried in vain to keep up with the Captain.

After looking for an hour or so for the rest of the Company, we went out in a pleasant grove near a spring and camped for the night. The army has not yet crossed the river, but all the wagons are over, a good sign that the army will soon follow.

Ate a late supper and fixing our humble bed beneath the thick leaves of a persimmon tree, we stretch out our wearied limbs for repose after a hard day's work, and most gratified it comes to us, for I feel secure here, and can rest without any fear of shell and shot from the enemy's artillery.

_____ *Wednesday July 6th* _____

Had a good breakfast this morning of Irish potatoes [and coffee] when we received orders to recross the river and join the balance of the Company. So after breakfast we recrossed on the Pontoon bridge and, turning to the left, went some mile or more to head Quarters. We there received Gen[eral] Stewart's farewell address to us as he has been promoted to Lieut[enant] Gen[eral] in place of Gen[eral] Pope [*sic*] killed in June [June 8, 1864] as recorded in my former volume.[11] After it, we cut out roads on line of battle. Received a package from Mobile containing books [and] cigars from my kind and attentive friend, Miss M[ary Jane Walker]. How pleasant to be remembered by absent friends.

_____ *Thursday 7th* _____

Was up and at work on a fort at the extreme left of our line. Finished the wood-work of it about noon, when we cut out a road for artillery leading to it which occupied us until dark as the hill was very steep and we had to cut it up in a diagonal direction. After we finished the road we crossed the river again and camped in our old place. Gen[eral Henry D.] Clayton, Gen[eral] Stewart's successor, celebrated his promotion to the Command of the Division by a heavy cannonading along the line. I think our artillery fired more cartridges in two hours than upon any day since the campaign.[12]

_____ *Friday 8th* _____

A lovely morning. Received orders to make a bomb-proof for Gen[eral] Clayton. After we finished it, we returned to Camp and rested the rest of the day. Towards night the shells from the enemy's battery nearly two miles distance commenced flying over us, so that we moved our Camp.13 We had a splendid supper, as I bought a q[uar]t of molasses and we had corn-meal cakes, stewed apples, bacon. Ate hearty.

_____ *Sat[urday] 9th* _____

Very hot. Moved to a new camp this morning and fixed up a good bed. Went out foraging and got a lot of apples, potatoes [et cetera]. Had another good supper.

_____ *Sunday July 10th* _____

Just at dark last night we received orders to move. It provoked me somewhat as I had taken some pains to fix up, expecting to remain here two or three days at least. Went down to the river and put straw weeds and bushes on the Pontoon bridge so that our artillery could cross without attracting the attention of the enemy. It was a sad sight to see our army moving silently across the river in the darkness of that July night. Brave fellows, they looked so down hearted as they filed silently by—it seems as though they had given up all hope of successfully holding the enemy at bay.14

Marched on towards Atlanta some four miles, when we halted and slept the balance of the night. Soon after daylight we came on another mile or so and camped for the rest of the day.

_____ *Monday 11th* _____

Left our camp of last night this morning and moved on about two miles where we camped in a thick wood, and by orders which we received I judge we will remain here several days, as it will take some time for the enemy to cross the river and until then we may expect a little rest.

We have had several showers to-day, [and] then sunshine.

*Tuesday, Wednesday, Thursday, Friday* and *Saturday* we remained in the same camp, the longest resting space we have had since we left the "Gap."[15]

―――――――――――― *Sunday 17th* ――――――――――――

Wrote several letters to-day for Mobile and other places. We have lived very well here and we went to town for some flour which we speedily converted into biscuit. About four o'cl[oc]k P.M. we received marching orders. Only went a mile or so and camped near our hospitals. I think the enemy are moving against our right, a few days will develope their movements. Learned that Gen[eral] Johnston is removed.[16]

―――――――――――― *Monday July 18th* ――――――――――――

Lovely weather now. Last night we had a full moon shining from a cloudless sky. Marched again this afternoon round to the right and camped after which are about three miles N[orth] E[ast] of Atlanta. We may expect hard work now until Atlanta falls. Gen[eral] Johnston is removed and Gen[eral] J[ohn] B[ell] Hood is now commanding in his stead. Do not like the change and I anticipate a bad effect therefore. Gen[eral] J[ohnston] has the confidence of his troops and I think they will fight under him better than any other commander.[17]

Bought a q[uar]t of syrup this morning and anticipate a good breakfast in the morning.

―――――――――――― *Tuesday 19th* ――――――――――――

Very hot day. Worked on artillery roads and bridges across Peachtree Creek all day. Heavy cannonading to our right.[18]

Road cut below West Point in Alabama. Thus I am cut off from Mobile, which does not please me at all, as all my correspondents are there.

—————————— *Wednesday 20th* ——————————

Detailed to go to the cook train to-day to do some work for H[ead] Quarters. Passed through the city, done our work and started back about four o'cl[oc]k. On reaching our camp we found it deserted. After much trouble and a good deal of inquiring, we learned the Division had moved to the right, so thither we wended our way.

After proceeding a mile or so we found a delightful blackberry thicket loaded with large luscious berries and stoped to eat a few.[19] Soon after the shells commenced whizzing over our heads. Sought a secure place where we remained until nearly dark, the balls and shells filling the air around us. About dark we found Fields, a member of our company, who piloted us to our camp, just in the rear of our line of battle. Delivered our work to H[ea]d Quarters, and upon inquiry learned that our baggage had been put in one of the H[ea]d Q[uarter]s wagons, and had gone no one knew where.[20]

—————————— *Thursday 21st* ——————————

At work cutting out roads this morning. Felt rather unwell. About noon we were ordered in to the breast works near the city. Slept in a house.

—————————— *Friday 22nd July* ——————————

Down to the right again, half-a-mile or so. Citizens living near the line have left their houses in great haste, leaving everything. One house directly in our "rear," a very neat gothic cottage, was left by the inmates early this morning, and it is now filled with soldiers, who are pillaging everything. One of my men got a blanket of white [word], very nice. Also several chicken. Went over and through the house. It was furnished in all the modern style of living, with a fine library, filled with a choice selection of books. The soldiers would come in and take a volume, without looking at it, thus setts of choice books were broken and scattered in every direction. Ladies dresses and garments of all kinds were scattered over the floor, fine crayon sketches were torn up. In fact, it made my heart sick to see such wanton destruction of property.[21]

About 2 o'cl[oc]k P.M. the hell opened again, and for two or three hours the battle raged with great fury. We charged the enemy's lines, and although we have cheering reunions, yet I do not think we have accomplished much. No doubt but we took about two thousand prisoners, yet our loss was heavy. Our lines still remain the same as before the fight. My Reg[imen]t was on picket and I do not think was in the charge. Hood will soon ruin his army at that rate. It will not do for the weaker army to charge the stronger. It will soon ruin the army. I care not how good fighting the material may be. We sleep to-night on our inner line of works and we had a very fine supper of peas.[22]

_____ *Saturday July 23rd* _____

Up before day, and cooked a fine breakfast. Had potatoes, peas and had plenty of bread with hog meat. Says Billie Mc[Mullen] when I made some remark about our cooking so much.—When we have plenty, cook plenty, "Because we can *hog*." I rejoined, "there is no use of making *hogs* of ourselves," to which Billie rejoined, "because we can *pack* there is no use of making *pack horses* of soldiers."

There is but little firing going on to-day, some artillery with shell and solid shot.

——————— *Sunday, Monday [and] Tuesday* ———————

We were at work on forts, lined well. Usual amount of cannonading along the lines.

——————— *Wednesday 27th* ———————

Moved again to-day and camped in town on Marietta St[reet]. Enemy moving to our left.[23] Another fight soon. Went over town until about midnight.

——————— *Thursday July 28th* ———————

Up and off early this morning to the Arsenal in the N[orth] W[est] part of the city. Here we rested until about 11 o'cl[oc]k when the whole army was moved rapidly to the left. We were ahead of all the infantry, and the first thing we knew, the cavalry fell back past us, and the balls falling around us showed that the enemy were near. Such confusion I never saw, the troops hurrying past us and forming in line of battle, while the continuous roar of musketry showed that they were hotly engaged. Falling back half-a-mile we stopped to await orders near the road, and I can truthfully say that I never saw so many wounded men in the same length of time before. It far exceeded the 28th of June.[24]

A few more such affairs as this and that of the 22nd and we will have no army left. This day's work has done more to demoralize our army than 3 months under Gen[era]l Johnston.

——————— *Friday 29th* ———————

Moved to the left a mile or so this morning, and camped near a fine large spring of excellent water. The troops formed a new line of battle, and of course, we had our hands full, cutting our roads. No fighting.[25]

_____ *Friday August 19th* _____

Our operations since the last record have been along our lines to East Point, the junction of the W[est] P[oint] and Atlanta and Macon road.[26] In the meantime we have lived well. Blackberries plenty. Bought a bushel of wheat and had it ground in flour this getting 32 lbs. for ten dollars. Also have had any amount of green corn. Have been blockading roads in the front of our left, where we found plenty of good foraging. We are now at East P[oin]t where we have been building forts and fortifying generally. Got my baggage all safe, except a few trifling articles the other day. For which, I was very truly thankful, as I had no change of clothing since they've been gone. This afternoon we received orders to go in the front of our left wing. Had rather dangerous times. We were only seperated from the enemy's advance line of skirmishers by one field.[27]

Came across a house in the woods, so to speak, whose sole occupant was a young woman and her infant child. She gave us a glass of buttermilk and we bought some chickens and potatoes from her. While engaged in cutting some trees, I disturbed a yellow jacket's nest and was stung severely in two or three places. Returned to our camp just before sundown, when we had the hardest thunderstorm of the season. The lightning was really vivid, while the rain fairly deluged the earth.

Managed to keep my things dry, but got wet myself in the arduous task. About dark it cleared off and proved to be a pleasant evening.

_____ *Monday August 22nd* _____

Yesterday we received orders about 2 ocl[oc]k to report to Corps H[ead] Q[uarters], for which I was not sorry as we were at work in the rain on breastworks for another Div[ision]. Camped at Utoy Church half a mile in rear of our line of battle, to the left of our Div[ision]. This morning we were ordered to make a lot of cheaveau-de-frize's for the protection of our line.

They are made something like a horse rack, consequently the boys have christened them by that name.[28]

Worked hard at it all day.

——————————————— *Wednesday 24th* ———————————————

Still at work on "racks." This afternoon we were at work in a ravine just to the rear of [General James T.] Holtzclaw's Brigade and one of the enemy's batteries was shelling the woods near us at a great rate.[29] Soon one of the pieces swept the ravine we were in. Most of the boys got behind trees, but thinking that one place was as good as another, I continued work. One of our boys, J. R. Wooten, got down behind a tree, and stopping to rest a few minutes, I went up [and] talked with him for a minute or two. Hurrying away, I had just resumed work when a solid shot whized past and hearing someone groan, I went to the tree and found the poor fellow gasping his last. The shot had struck him in the left side or hip, tore off his left thigh, his left arm, and his right leg below the knee. His death was almost instanteous. We carried him up the side of the hill, and getting a blanket, we carried him down to our camp, where we made a rough coffin and buried him as well as we could. It was a consolation at all events to know that his grave is marked and that he was buried in a civilized manner.

——————————————— *Saturday August 27th* ———————————————

The Yanks all left our front last night. Soon after breakfast went out to level down their works across the road so that our cavalry can get out and see what they are doing. Some new stratagem of Sherman's, I suppose. We'll see. Nearly all the boys think they are retreating and are highly elated with the idea.[30] All Bosh! Had a fine time roaming over their camp getting crackers and bacon. Captured a fine sutler's wagon which was filled with goods, but did not get any of them as [General Randall L.] Gibson's Brigade plundered it before we got there.[31]

_____ *Sunday August 28th* _____

What a lovely day. After putting on some clean clothes this morning, I went over to the Yank's works. Saw [Lucius] Potter of the 36th [Alabama Regiment] and passed the forenoon with him.[32] Sherman's plans are not yet developed nor will they be until too late I think. Hood's ordeal has arrived, he will either make for himself a name that will live or he will be remembered only to be derided. It is the *tide* in his affairs, and I think he will fail. A few more days, perhaps hours, will decide his fate.[33]

_____ *Wednesday August 31st* _____

The ordeal is past and J[ohn] B[ell] Hood is gone under. Went to East P[oin]t yesterday morning, remained there all day, and this morning early came down to Jonesboro. Our infantry reached here, and charged the enemy in their works as usual, only to be repulsed with heavy loss. This horrid useless waste of human life, this wholesale butchery is terrible and should damn the authors through all time.[34]

Our company reached the place just as the fight commenced, but did not see much of it. Had a hearty laugh at one of our Lieutenants, who was carrying a musket and teakettle. Directly a shell burst near him and away went the gun while he struck out in a dog trot. A few minutes after another shell bursted and a piece or rather spent fragment struck him on the leg, when away went the teakettle and away went the Lieutenant, who was seen no more until we were far out of danger. Thank God, I have stronger nerves than that.

Our boys have been repulsed all along the line, and I see it requires no military man to tell that Atlanta is gone.

_____ *Thursday September 1st* _____

The great struggle is over. Atlanta is being incinerated. Our [General Stephen D. Lee's] Corps was put in motion early this morning to march towards the city and cover the retreat of

Stewart's Corps while [General William J.] Hardee was left at Jonesboro to hold the forces there in check. The troops are already demoralized and such straggling I never saw before.[35]

Proceeded to within five miles of Atlanta where we camped. Stewart's Corps is busy destroying stores in the city and report says will leave to-night.[36]

Well I am heartily glad of it and if it had been evacuated six weeks ago it would have been better.

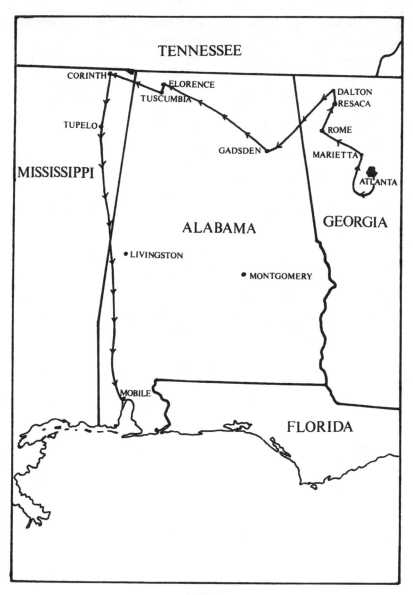

MAP 4.
## Atlanta to Mobile
SEPTEMBER–NOVEMBER 1864

# 5

# Retreat from Atlanta

SEPTEMBER 2 TO NOVEMBER 14, 1864

## Friday 2nd

Retreated towards McDonough, Billie McMullen [and] myself concluded we would straggle some and try [and] get something fresh [and] good to eat. Took a road running parallel with the McDonough road and had the good fortune to get a good dinner and excellent supplies. Our supplies consisted of good biscuit, milk, butter, honey and pies. We done it ample justice as the reader of these pages may depend. We overtook the Division after dark [and] camped in a pine thicket.[1]

Indications of rain.

## Sunday 4th of September

At last, I hope we have a little resting spell. We are near Jonesboro and the enemy has fallen back towards Atlanta.[2]

We are camped in a very good county and I anticipate some good foraging here, as honey and mutton is plenty. Also plenty of sugar cane and some sweet potatoes, just getting in eating order.

Have fixed up a very good camp and don't care if we remain here a month or two or as long as the war lasts. Brought in a fine bee hive to-night. 40 lbs. of excellent honey.

—————————————— *Sat[urday] 17th* ——————————————

Up and off by daylight this morning. Have got a good rest—over a week. Took up our line of March for the Rail-Road, crossed it about a mile when we camped for the day. Is this the inciting step of a new campaign? I am inclined to think it is.[3]

—————————————— *Sun[day] 18th* ——————————————

Up [and] off again this morning by daylight. Had a hard day's march of it. Reached Flat-Rock church about an hour after dark when we camped, ahead of the whole army.[4]

—————————————— *Monday 19th* ——————————————

The troops commenced passing about 8 o'cl[oc]k, and about nine we received orders to go ahead of the whole army again. One and a-half divisions were ahead of us, and to one who has tried to get ahead of a lot of troops, the task will be known to be no light one. It was the hardest march on record. Roads were very bad, and I soon got tired down, but kept on however, determined never to give it up so. Reached the W[est] P[oin]t road and passed through the little town of Palmetto, four miles beyond to a store on road called Petersburg. Several sweet potato fields lined the road and we managed to lay in a good supply. They say we will lay here several days.[5]

Hope so for this trip short as it is has completely broke me down.

—————————————— *Thursday Sept[ember] 29th* ——————————————

We have had another good resting spell and have lived pretty well while we were resting. Was in hopes I could get off to Mobile to rejoin my command but have not as yet.

Received orders soon after dinner to get ready to move. Jeff Davis has been here to review us and we have all sorts of rumors. I think we are bound for Tenn[essee].[6]

About four o'cl[oc]k we finally got off, marching towards the Chatahoochee River. Marched an hour or so after dark. Camped within four miles of the River. Army in better spirits than they were.[7]

_____ *Monday Oct[ober] 3rd* _____

Once more in the vicinity of Lost M[ountain] and the Kenesaw. It seemed to me in marching here that we have gone three miles to get ahead one. Such a crooked route I never saw.

Stewart's Corps is cutting the R[ail] R[oad] and playing the devil generally if we are to believe half we hear. Have had the usual amount of work to do on roads and battle-lines. Rain, rain, rain. I do wonder if it ever stops raining here? It was raining all last summer when we were here, and raining yet. Have got a good many chesnuts here. Boiled them, reminds me of old times.[8]

_____ *Thursday Oct[ober] 6th* _____

We are camped in the little town of Dallas to-night, a place that will ever be made memorable from the fact that the battle of New Hope Church was fought only a mile or two distant. We passed over the battle field to-day. The trees were scarred where the balls penetrated them, while thousands of branches, cut by balls so that they hung down [and] died drooped from every tree showing that but few balls fired during a battle take effect. I begin to see now why it is that so few persons are killed, there is so much wild shooting.[9]

_____ *Saturday Oct[ober] 8th* _____

Our company left Van Wert M[ountain] last night about 2 o'cl[oc]k and marched all night towards Cedar Point, blazing the road the army was to pass the next day, and cutting out logs. It was a hour's night march, sometimes wading creeks up to our waist.[10] Passed through a potato patch and secured a valuable acquisition to our commissaries in the shape of sweet potatoes. Stoped an hour before day and built a roaring fire. Roasted potatoes and dried ourselves. I shall never forget that night's march. It was full of incidents that will ever live in my mind.

After dinner, we pursued our way, reaching Cedar Point about 10 o'cl[oc]k. Eat breakfast at a private house. Very good with Mike Collery, as good an Irishman as ever walked. At Cedar P[oin]t we rested several hours until our troops came up, then went on eight miles as far as Cedar Creek, where we camped for the night. Cedar Creek is a good sized stream and although cold, most of the troops waded it. Rather a laughable incident occurred here. As [Colonel A. M.] Manigault's Brigade were marching down with pants and drawers off to cross it, a young fellow with a young lady came along in a buggy and she had to see about two thousand half naked rebs. "Phancy her pheelings."[11]

This morning, Sunday 9th, we built a foot bridge across the river then came on to Cave Spring where we rested two hours for our Division to come up. After which we pursued our way over a very good road as far to another two miles or so of the river. It was a clear lovely night, only rather cold. Allen got some fine sweet potatoes, very large and very good. Roasted a few and ate them, then went to bed in a corn crib, on good soft corn husks.

—————————— *Monday 10th* ——————————

Crossed the Coosa River this morning at Quinn's ferry, some ten miles below Rome. Marched over a wild mountainous road and rugged country some 13 miles where we camped for the night.[12]

—————————— *Tuesday 11th* ——————————

Led the army to-day. Hard work. Camped at 2 o'cl[oc]k. Enemy beyond the Oostanaula River.[13]

—————————— *Wednesday 12th* ——————————

Up and off this morning at 3 o'cl[oc]k. Reached the river at daylight. Threw the Pontoon bridge across and crossed over soon after. Some of the troops went to Calhoun five miles distant. Brought back some few prisoners and plenty of plunder.[14]

—————————— *Thursday 13th* ——————————

Left camp last night about midnight. Came on to within four or five miles of Resaca. Camped inside the Yankee breastworks of last spring, near Snake Creek gap. Cut down a chesnut tree and had a good *feast* of chesnuts. Rested the rest of the day, and we are having lovely fall weather now. On every side of us are evidences of last spring's campaign—breastworks, old camps and soldiers' graves.[15]

—————————— *Friday 14th* ——————————

Have been blockading roads across Adam's M[ountain] all day. Very wild and romantic. The valley beyond is called the "pocket." People living there have never been out of it they say.

—————————— *Sat[urday] 15th* ——————————

Blockading Snake Creek gap all last night and this morning.[16] Hard work. After a hard day's march we camped on a pleasant creek where we had [an] abundance of sweet potatoes. Had [a] fine supper.

—————————— *Mon[day] 17th* ——————————

Rested nearly all day yesterday. Today we marched early and passed through Summerville about noon. Camped near the state line.[17]

—————————— *Wednesday 19th* ——————————

In Alabama we move, near Pelve Road. Great sweet potatoes. Our men lay in about four bushels. Received my first mail to-day for a long time. Letters from Miss M[ary] J[ane] W[alker] and Serg[ean]t P. S. G.[18]

────────────── *Friday 21st* ──────────────

Reached Gadston [Gadsden] on the Coosa River about noon. Camped half-a-mile below town near the river. Received a mail. Got a lot of papers from Mobile. Drew clothing of which I was in much need.[19]

────────────── *Saturday 22nd* ──────────────

Left at 3 o'cl[oc]k P.M. and crossed Black Creek 2 miles from town, rendered somewhat conspicuous in this war by an exploit of [Nathan Bedford] Forrest. Here is where [Colonel A. D.] Str[e]ight crossed and burned the bridge. Forrest was piloted over by a young girl [Emma Sansom] living in the vicinity and captured Str[e]ight.[20]

We crossed by the same ford. Built fires near there and remained until 9 o'clock or thereabouts. Then went on half-a-mile beyond and camped. Very cold. We are now I think on our way to Linn.[21]

────────────── *Sun[day] 23rd* ──────────────

Off at daylight this morning. Made a big days march and camped near the head of the Warren River at a great Spring.

────────────── *Mon[day] 24th* ──────────────

Left [at] daylight. Marched 23 miles ahead of Pontoon train. Passed through Brooksville and Summit, ascended Sand M[ountain].[22] Took supper at Mrs. Moon's. Hospitable.

────────────── *Tuesday 25th* ──────────────

Miserable poor country. Made about 12 miles. Descended Sand M[ountain], just at dusk. Camped at the foot in [a] peach grove.[23]

_____ *Wednesday 26th* _____

Rained last night. Awful muddy to-day. Country very rough and poor. Went out foraging. Got nothing. Had a fine camp and built a big fire. Passed through Summerville. Mud shoe mouth deep.

_____ *Thursday 27th* _____

Capt[ain] Oliver [and] Lieut[enant] Grimley were arrested last night and this morning we had two new officers over us. Lieut[enant] Cesare and Lieut[enant] De Graffenreid.24 Had a long and hard days march. Never saw so many persimmons in my life. Eat some. Very fine area. Camped in a big wood, after making 18 miles.

_____ *Friday Oct[ober] 28th* _____

Left camp at nine o'cl[oc]k this morning. After a march of 16 miles we struck the Tenn[essee] River bottom. The bottom is as fine a country as I ever saw, but this war has played havoc with it. Great farms all going to ruin. Saw a fine house off to the left. Went to it with Carroll. Got nothing. "Given away to soldiers all they had." Certainly! Camped near an overseer's house. Had plenty of Begars [*sic*] come to *charm*.

_____ *Sat[urday] 29th* _____

Cloudy this morning. Left at 5 o'cl[oc]k. Marched through Cortland. Fine place before the war. Going to ruin now. R[ail] R[oad] all tore up.25 Bridges down below. Made 16 miles.

_____ *Sun[day] 30* _____

Off at 5 o'cl[oc]k again. Beautiful roads. Great corn field and pea field. Laid in a supply. Stoped within a mile of the river. Went to work putting in Pontoon bridges in front of Florence. Exciting times. Heavy cannonading. Last troops crossed over.

Eat a good supper off of pears. Crossed over just at dark. Go up in town. Get asked to tea with some ladies.[26]

_____ *Monday 31st* _____

Eat breakfast at Mrs. Hugh Thomas's, Miss Maggie Shannon, Miss Laura. Eat supper at same place. Pleasant evening. Feel better after it.

_____ *Sund[ay] Nov[ember] 6th* _____

At last I have orders to go to Mobile to rejoin my command.[27] It cheers me up. Called on Mrs. T[homas]. The past week I have been building forts [and] throwing the Pontoon bridge across the river.

_____ *Mon[day] 7th* _____

Got ready to start for Mobile at 2 o'cl[oc]k. Sorry to leave the boys, some of which I have formed a warm attachment for. Goodbye Billie [McMullen]. Hope to meet in better days.

Crossed the river and made a night march to Tuscumbia. Great spring at that place. Rain. Slept under an old shed.[28]

_____ *Tuesday 8th* _____

Off at day light. Creek up. Cut tree across it. Fell in water. Pretty wet. Reach wagon yard. Leave for Cherokee. Awful road. Rain. R[ail] R[oad] tore up.[29] Reached Cherokee at dark. Drew rations. Left for a depot two miles before to sleep. Had a good night's rest. Plenty of room [and] fire.

_____ *Wed[nesday] 9th* _____

Another rainy day. Left C[herokee] at 2 o'cl[oc]k P.M. on train. Made slow time. Tracks cleared off just before sunset. Reached Corinth at 8 o'cl[oc]k at night.

## _Sunday Nov[ember] 13th_

Corinth, the grave-yard of Mississippi, as it has aptly been called, is far different from the Corinth of three years ago. The different armies that have operated there and in the vicinity have defaced the country so that one acquainted with the place two years or so ago would scarcely recognize a single point, unless some of the buildings in town. I passed the day on Thursday roaming over the battle field looking at the forts, breastworks and so on. One of my camp [mates] was in the battle of Corinth, and as he was charging one of the forts, fell with eleven wounds in his breast. We stood at the point and under his guidance went through with all the different movements of our forces.[30]

We bought a lot of flour and baked a lot of biscuit[s], so that we lived well, and have enough left to last us most of the way to Mobile. Left C[orinth] on Friday morning at 8 o'clock. It was a lean [and] cold day. Reached West P[oint] at dark. Bought a few sweet potatoes and had a fine supper.

Some of the boys left us there for Pickens C[ounty], Ala-[bama].

It was a lovely night, clear and a full moon. Slept in a church at night.

Next day, Saturday, we left at 6 o'cl[oc]k. Reached Meridian at 4 P.M. I intended to remain there and go up the central road and pay [Joshua J.] Aughe a visit at Livingston, but found it very uncertain when a train would leave, so I kept on down to Mobile. Trainded all night and reach[ed] M[obile] this morning at 9 o'cl[oc]k. Went up home. Mrs. B[randt] did not know me at first. Washed and put on some clean clothes. This P.M. called on Miss W[alker]. Mrs. T[urner] came to the door but did not recognize me until I spoke. She introduced me as Mr. Smith to Miss W[alker] and son.[31]

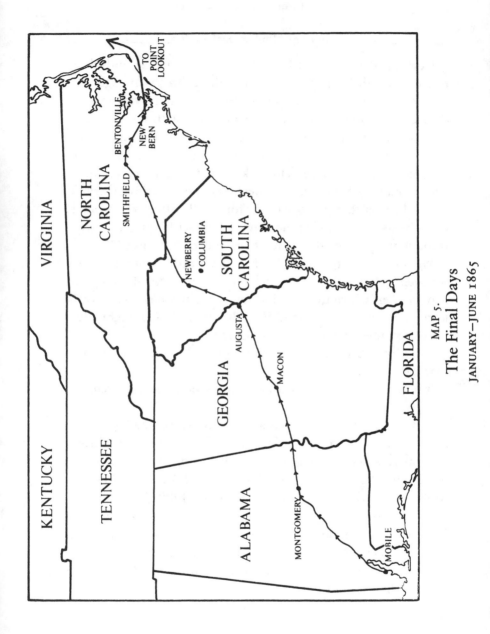

KENTUCKY

TENNESSEE

VIRGINIA

NORTH CAROLINA

BENTONVILLE

NEW BERN

SMITHFIELD

TO POINT LOOKOUT

NEWBERRY

COLUMBIA

SOUTH CAROLINA

GEORGIA

AUGUSTA

MACON

ALABAMA

MONTGOMERY

FLORIDA

MOBILE

MAP 5.
The Final Days
JANUARY–JUNE 1865

# 6

# From Mobile to
# Point Lookout Prison

JANUARY 29 TO APRIL 26, 1865

At this point, H. S. Williams does not record events that hap-
pened during his stay with Confederate forces in Mobile. On
January 22, 1865, however, he received permission to visit the
city for personal reasons. One week later, Williams and the 40th
Alabama Regiment were ordered to rejoin the Army of Tennessee in South Carolina. Included below is a copy of the pass
that allowed him to return to the city.[1]

Camp 40th Ala[bama] Inf[an]try
Jan[uary] 22nd, 1865

Captain [William E.] Yancey:[2]
Sir:
   You will confer a great favor on Mr. Williams by
approving his pass for 12 hours even. His effects are all in the
City of Mobile and he is very anxious to fix up things
Suitable to leave for a considerable length of time, the
uncertainty of our forces being able to hold the city make it
more important for him to have the privilege of a pass.
   by so complying you will confere a favor on your
humble Ser[van]t

T. M. Brunson
Capt[ain] Co[mpany] "C"[3]

Williams resumes his diary a week later.

On Sunday morning Jan 29, 1865, my Reg[imen]t left Mobile on the St[eamer] St. Charles for Montgomery on our way to S[outh] C[arolina].4 The boat was crowded too much for comfort, yet we got along very well. River very high. Reached M[ontgomery] about sundown. Next morning we left for Columbus, Ga. and the R[ail] R[oad]. Reached C[olumbus] about 8 o'cl[oc]k. Thursday morning we left for Macon. Reached M[acon] at 4 o'cl[oc]k P.M. The Reg[iment] went on to Milledgeville, but Spud [Benson] and myself got left. Spent the night in town. Called on Capt[ain] Crisp [and] family.5 Went to the Theatre. Came on to Milledgeville next morning, where we found the Reg[iment]. Left M[illedgeville] on Saturday for Augusta. Had a gap of 36 miles to walk. Passed through Sparta on Sunday. Monday we reached Mayfield and took the train for Camack on the Augusta and Atlanta R[ail] R[oad].6

It was an awful night [and] I took a severe cold by being exposed to the storm. Reached Augusta next day just before dark. Drew rations and marched across the river [and] four miles East after dark.7 Remained in the vicinity of this place until the morning of the 15th instant, when we took up our line of march for Columbia [South Carolina].8

_____ *Thursday Feb[ruary] 16th* _____

Made 16 miles to-day over a sandy and rather poor country.

_____ *Fri[day] 17* _____

The enemy have Columbia so we turned off and are now going towards Newberry [North Carolina], 18 miles.9

—————————————— *Sat[urday] 18* ——————————————

Reached Frog Land at noon [and] camped 2 miles beyond near the R[ail] R[oad].

—————————————— *Sun[day] 19* ——————————————

Marched 6 miles to Newberry C[ourt] H[ouse] where we found a line of battle. [General Judson] Killpatrick's cavalry are on our right they say. Monday rested all day. Good foraging— flour, potatoes.[10]

—————————————— *Tues[day] 21st* ——————————————

Left at sunrise for Chester. The Brigade marched 24 miles, but I fell out after going 9 miles in company with three others. Camped in the woods and rested the balance of the day.

—————————————— *Wed[nesday] 22nd* ——————————————

Seen some troops come marching back this morning. On inquiry found it to be our boys returning. Fall in and went back. Camped near a sick old fellows sweet potatoes [and] sorghum.

—————————————— *Thurs[day] 23rd* ——————————————

Our Brigade came up this morning. Joined them and went on to Newberry. Took the train for Pomania [Pomaria] 15 miles below here. Camped in a thick wood. Dull and rainy. Miserable weather.[11]

—————————————— *Fri[day] 26* ——————————————

Rain all day. Awful bad lightning. Bad humour.

—————————————— *Sat[urday] 25th* ——————————————

Same as yesterday. Smoke has nearly blinded me.

―――――――――――― *Sun[day] 26* ――――――――――――

Left at noon for Chester again. Waded creek. Roads almost impassable. Marched 7 miles.

―――――――――――― *Mon[day] 27th* ――――――――――――

Horrible roads. Camped within two miles of the Enoree River.[12]

―――――――――――― *Tues[day] 28* ――――――――――――

Crossed the river and camped. [Frank] Sims [and] myself went out foraging.[13] Got 15 lbs. of flour, half a bushel of potatoes, two canteens of syrup, 3 lbs of lard, chicken and a peck of corn meal, all for two dollars. Good luck. Had a fine dinner too at Mr. Browning's. Very clever. In fact best country to soldier in of any I ever struck.

―――――――――――― *Wed[nesday March] 1st* ――――――――――――

Off soon after sunrise. Roads horrible too bad for description. Carried several small [streams] with mud up to my knees. Horrible!

―――――――――――― *Thurs[day] 2nd* ――――――――――――

Another horrible day. Crossed Broad River at dark and camped a mile beyond.[14]

―――――――――――― *Sat[urday] 4th* ――――――――――――

Off again in the rain. Spud Benson [and] myself fell out.[15] Took dinner at Mrs. Hardwicks. Mrs. Mollie. Fine evening. Excellent dinner. Had a good time generally. Slept at a private house in grand bed. Felt first rate, after a good supper.

―――――――――――― *Sun[day] 5* ――――――――――――

Reached Chester this morning about 10 o'cl[oc]k. Found Reg[iment].[16]

—————————— *Saturday March 18th/65* ——————————

Since last record we came on to Salisbury, N[orth] C[arolina] on R[ail] R[oad]. Remained there two or three days, then came on to Raleigh, where we remained over night, then on to Smithfield by R[ail] R[oad], near which we joined our old (Clayton's) Division on yesterday. This morning we move off for Bentonville early and after one of the hardest day's march on record we camped two miles beyond in a heavy wood.

The weather is very pleasant, and I am tired enough to appreciate a good night's rest. Should not be surprised if we were not in a fight ere long.

—————————— *Sunday March 19th* ——————————

This morning we were moved out with great caution and about ten o'clock were formed in line of battle some three miles below Bentonville. A few shells flew around us, but the level nature of the country does not admit of the using of artillery, for which I feel thankful. Slight skirmishing commenced soon after we got in line, and soon after the Yanks made a charge on our first line, but were repulsed with loss. We hastily constructed rough log breastworks, but were not permitted to use them.[17]

About 12 o'cl[oc]k we were ordered to attention and soon afterward moved forward. It required no experienced eye to see that we had to charge the enemy. An hour afterward we were ordered over our front line of breastworks to support our first line of battle. In an hour we moved slowly forward, while our first line drove the enemy steadily back. The first line then lay down while we jumped over them and rushed to the charge with great impetuosity. We drove them back carrying [the] enemy line of breastworks with great rapidity and with heavy loss.[18]

Their line in our front gave way and we pursued them through the low pine swamps for a mile or so, completely flanking the works on our left. With some few others I made my way up in the rear of their works. Our loss here was heavy, yet if

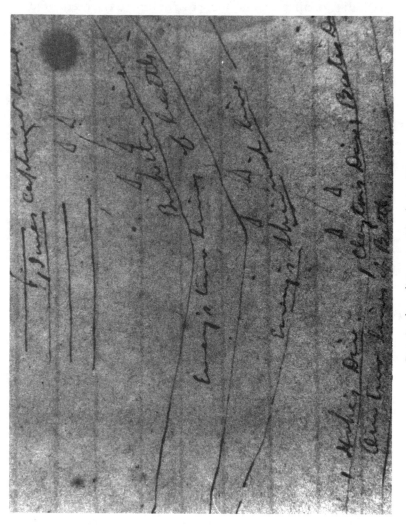

Drawing from diary entry, March 19, 1865

we had only been supported, we could have captured the whole Corps with which we were engaged, but our reserve failed to come up. Also [Major General Robert Frederick] Hoke's Division in first, so that we were compelled to give way. As I had no idea of going back, I lay down below our breastworks and was captured about an hour by [the] sun by the 14[th Corps] A[rmy of the] C[umberland].[19]

They gave us credit for fighting them as hard as they were ever fought and some told me it was the first time their line was ever broken. Some thought we had whiskey to incite us on. Quite a compliment. I will draw a rough map of the field.

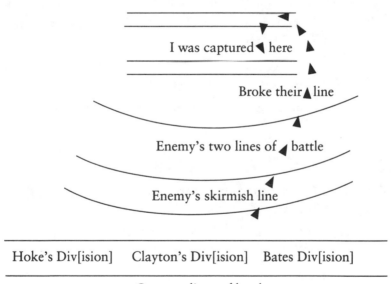

Five others besides myself in my company were captured, and saw 49 out of my Brigade, 28 out of my Reg[iment]. We were kept on the battle field until dark, then marched to the rear where we camped for the night. It is a clear beautiful night and I feel well after my hard and arduous day's work. We are guarded by an Michigan Reg[iment] who captured us. I am anxious to learn how the boys came out. Our company up to the time I left it suffered worse than in any battle it was ever in. We lost two killed dead and some 7 wounded. What its loss was after that I have no means of knowing.

—————————— *Monday 20th* ——————————

Moved first to the Division, then to Corps H[ead] Quarters.

—————————— *Tues[day] 21st* ——————————

Left this P.M. in the rain for H[ead] Q[uarters] of the 20[th Corps] A[rmy of the] C[umberland] then were moved off with all the prisoners, saw 800, towards Goldsboro. Muddy tramp. Wet [and] cold. No rations.

—————————— *Wed[nesday] 22nd* ——————————

Clear and quite pleasant. Marched all day over a very good road.

—————————— *Thurs[day] 23rd* ——————————

Reached Goldsboro to-day at 10 o'clock. Passed through and took the Kinston road.

—————————— *Fri[day] 24th* ——————————

Reached Kinston at 2 o'cl[oc]k. Drew rations for the first time since we were captured of any account. Crossed river and camped.[20]

—————————— *Sat[urday] 25th* ——————————

Left K[inston] at ten o'clock last night. Reached New Bern at 3 o'cl[oc]k this morning. At ten were marched in the jail yard. Lovely weather. Changed to a new jail yard last evening.

_____ *Sun[day] 26* _____

Cold and disagreeable.

_____ *Mon[day] 27* _____

Left this evening at 5 o'cl[oc]k on Steamship "Fairbanks."

_____ *Fri[day] 31st* _____

Reached Ft. Hateras this morning at daylight. Lay there all day. Got off at noon on Wednesday. Heavy sea. Sea sick. Reached Fortress Monroe on Thursday at 1 o'cl[oc]k. Left for Point Lookout. Reached there on Friday [and] left ship at 2 o'cl[oc]k P.M. Went in the Camp at dark. *In Prison. Rather hard.*[21]

_____ *Monday 10th of April* _____

Received a letter from my Brother this evening. Have not had anything do me as much good for a long time. Will be out here ere long. All well he says.

_____ *Friday April 21st* _____

It seems impossible to get any money here. Have not received a cent from brother yet. Others who came here with me and who had friends in the North have heard from them in the shape of 20 [and] 30 dollars in greenbacks, but narie a cent have I. This is hard, but I look for one every day, "tomorrow and tomorrow and tomorrow."[22]

_____ *Wednesday April 26th* _____

This prison life is getting unendurable. The weary monotony of day after day, it is awful. Were I situated as I wish to be, I could not get along better, but as it is, I dread the coming of each day. Had I a wood house as some have, with money enough to buy what I dearly need, both food and clothing, I could content myself, but instead, not a dollar have I got as yet, and we have a small hut in which five of us have to sleep on the ground and the wind here is fairly alive with rumors that trouble us terribly.[23]

How long is this state of things to continue? Not long I hope, yet there is no telling. For a week past I have been looking for and expecting money from my brother, but not a line have I had, nor a dollar. Why it is I cannot imagine. Has he not received my last letters, or is he afraid to risk a few dollars. Had I ten dollars in Greenbacks I could get along very well, as I could buy as much clothing and food as I wanted. Even had I something to read I could get along very well, but even a paper is a rarity.[24]

# 7

# Sayings of Madam Rumor

APRIL 10 TO JUNE 6, 1865

[Note: The following are jumbled entries made by H. S. Williams during his incarceration. Dates are juxtaposed, and rumors and reports of daily activities are intertwined. The editor has organized these entries according to dates listed.]

## Sayings of Madam Rumor

### Ap[ri]l 10th

Lincoln killed in theatre at Washington. Some say Richmond—*per Mr. Sims*. Not so, Gen[era]l Baker, formerly commander of this post, killed and not Lincoln. Flags at halfmast.—10,000 prisoners to be paroled out of this camp.—Lincoln made a proposition for the South to keep what negroes she wants at 5 dollars per month, clothe themselves.—Rations to be increased, 1½ loafs, 2 days. All C[onfederate] S[tates] soldiers between the ages of 18 [and] 35 to take the oath, and form a reserve corps from which the U.S. armies are to be recruited. All under 18 [and] over 35 to become free [and] return to their respective homes. *Pvt. Warner.* England has recognized the C[onfederate] States. Just heard that Booth the tragedian was playing at the Washington

Theatre and in a stage duel shot his pistol off, which was loaded, the ball taking effect in Mr. Lincoln producing instant death.[1]

────────────── *April 16th* ──────────────

The camp's full of rumors this morning concerning the death of Lincoln. All agree that he was shot at the Washington Theatre.—Maj[or] Brady, Pro[vost] Marshal gone to Washington to see about getting a lot of us out of here. (Pvt. Coleman) Going to parole us or commence at least to-morrow.[2]

—Gent went to get a permit for clothing, but Maj[or] Barnes told him not to trouble himself about sending as he would be away from here before they could arrive.[3]

Not only is Lincoln killed, but Seward is stabbed, also his son, and Lincoln's son Bob.[4]

—5,000 prisoners to go out of here to-morrow. All living inside of the Federal lines—Seward dead [and] nobody else.— 3,000 men to be drawn for and shot in this prison as retaliation. Oh my!—Grant advises the parole of all prisoners.[5]

────────────── *April 17th* ──────────────

Lee sent a [words] to Gen[era]l Johnston to advise him to surrender.

—[General Benjamin F.] Butler [and Andrew] Johnston conspired against Lincoln [and] had him assassinated. B[utler] in confinement. Johnston fled. [He meant Andrew Johnson.]

Maj[or] Brady has returned from Washington with orders to parole us, but owing to Lincoln's assassination they are now countermanded. Supposed to be only temporarily.

—All the prisoners who came in here after the 25th of March are to be sent to Elmira, N[ew] Y[ork].[6]

—Gen[era]l Lee arrested and held as a hostage for the murder of L[incoln].

_____ *April 19th* _____

Yesterday passed off with out any rumors. Strange!

—Maj[or] Brady telegraphed to Washington as to his course, and received an answer to go to paroling. So says rumor in the shape of a Mr. D. in the hospital.—

Mobile surrendered with 7,000 prisoners. Also Johnston and [Colonel John S.] Mosby have surrendered on the same conditions as Lee. Great excitement.[7]

Mobile certainly gave up. Johnston at last account about to surrender on same conditions as Lee. Mosby surrendered. We will be paroled in a few days.[8]

_____ *April 20th* _____

They will commence paroling to-morrow all who were captured previous to the 25th of March.—Mobile is certainly gone up. The city with 5,000 men and Spanish Fort with 500 men.[9]

_____ *April 21st* _____

[Joseph E.] Johnston certainly surrendered. Johnston (Andy) says the leaders of the rebellion must suffer. The *deluded* followers will soon be sent to their homes.

—Gen[eral Richard S.] Ewell sent to Ft. Deleware.[10]

—Everyday there are more or less rumors about paroling. Every day we stay here that the good work will certainly commence to-morrow. Amen! [And] may that morrow soon come, for I'm tired of this place.

[General Edmund] Kirby Smith surrendered in Mississippi.[11]

_____ *April 22nd* _____

Great plot among negro troops in Charleston and the negroes about town. Plot discovered [and] 30 niggers killed.[12]

—More rumors about parole. Commence Monday morning certainly. Jeff[erson] Davis taken command of Johnston's army, and says he will fight the war to the bitter end.[13]

——————————————— *April 23rd* ———————————————

Gen[era]l Johnston would not surrender, so his men have all disbanded and are going home. Jeff[erson] Davis was at Greensboro, N[orth] C[arolina] [and] could not keep them together.[14]

——————————————— *April 25th* ———————————————

Johnston surrendered to Sherman with the priviledge of turning all the armies over to State authorities. Government would not recognize it. Of Course not! Also—a teacher here about to start a school went to Gen[era]l Barnes to see about it, [and] said if he [we] were going to be paroled soon he would not commence, whereupon Gen[era]l B[arnes] told him to commence.

——————————————— *April 26th* ———————————————

France [and] Mexico formed an alliance with C[onfederate] S[tates] and landed 13,000 men in the South.—Gen[era]l Barnes says we'll certainly be paroled ere long, say a month or so, at least. Very good![15]

——————————————— *April 27th* ———————————————

Maj[or] Brady says we'll certainly be paroled, commencing to-morrow. Good, if so! But there's been too many rumors to that effect.

——————————————— *[April] 28th* ———————————————

Dr. Crause says that they are paroling all prisoners in the hospital captured previous to April 1. *Hatten.*

——————————————— *May 2nd* ———————————————

All humbug! To-day we all registered our names to take the oath of allegiance. I do not think 20 men out of 20,000 refused to register. "They say" we'll be out of here in a week's time.

—————————————— *May 8th* ——————————————

Blockade runners went out yesterday. Rumor says all the ABCs will go out [and] take the oath to-day. I think they will go out by States. Hope to be in N[ew] Y[ork] by one-[and]-a-half weeks at least.

—————————————— *June 6th* ——————————————

The one [and] a half weeks has assumed gigantic proportions. Nearly a month, [and] I am yet here. Cleaning out Hospitals now. Hope to get out ere long, say in two weeks.[16]

# Notes

## Introduction

1. Francis Bazley Lee, *Genealogical and Memorial History of the State of New Jersey* (New York: Lewis Historical Publishing Co., 1910), 1221–61.

2. *The New York Coachmakers Magazine,* Volume 4, Number 9, May 1862, 137–38.

3. Ibid.

4. Printed letter, E. B. Barlett to Thomas M. Ford, April 29, 1856. Petition for reinstatement to the Ohio Council of the American Order, March 20, 1856. See also, State Council of Ohio charter granted to Madison, Ohio, council with Hiram S. Williams, James H. Dwyer, and James H. Wigginton listed as officers and issued on May 27, 1856. All primary source materials are in the possession of Williams' granddaughter, Mrs. Margaret Williams Rainwater, Rockledge, Florida, and are hereafter referred to as the Rainwater Collection.

5. Undated printed copies of travel accounts and political activities in H. S. Williams Scrapbook and twelve unpublished diaries for the years 1853–1858. Rainwater Collection. J. H. Wigginton accompanied Williams on his journeys.

6. *The New York Coachmakers Magazine,* Volume 4, Number 9, April 1862, 138.

7. Commonplace book entry, Volume "1858," 25. Rainwater Collection.

8. *The New York Coachmakers Magazine,* Volume 4, Number 9, May 1862, 138.

9. Undated entry, Williams Travel Diary for 1856. Rainwater Collection.

10. Commonplace book entry, Volume "1858," 25. Rainwater Collection.

11. Ezra M. Stratton to H. S. Williams, March 5, 1861. Rainwater Collection.

12. Ezra M. Stratton to H. S. Williams, February 23, 1861. Rainwater Collection.

13. Ezra M. Stratton to H. S. Williams, March 5, 1861. Rainwater Collection.

14. Muster roll for Company C, March 15, 1861. State of Alabama Department of Archives and History. This roll does not show Williams as a member. See Samuel Henry Sprott, "Sumter in the Civil War," *Our Southern Home,* 1899. Sprott lists Henry S. Williams as a member of Company C. Photocopy in possession of editors.

15. Clement A. Evans, ed., *Confederate Military History* (Atlanta: Confederate Publishing Co., 1899), Volume VII, 180–83.

16. D. H. Sadler to "All Royal Arch Masons Throughout the Globe," December 3, 1863. Rainwater Collection. Williams remained a Mason throughout his life, and when he relocated to Florida in 1874, he brought with him letters of introduction from the Demopolis, Alabama, lodge. See Membership Certificate, August 1, 1867; member certification letter, November 16, 1867; and Membership Certificate, June 17, 1863. Rainwater Collection.

17. Diary entry, February 16, 1864. See also petition for transfer into Confederate Navy, February 10, 1864. Photocopy in possession of editors. Mobile *Register and Advertiser,* October 13, 1863.

18. Diary entry, February 16, 1864.

19. Ibid., March 10, 1864.

20. Ibid.

21. Ibid., May 27, 1864.

22. Ibid. For an extended examination of the impact of the horrors of war on the psyche of Civil War soldiers, see Reid Mitchell, *Civil War Soldiers* (New York: Viking Penquin, 1988); James I. Robertson, Jr., *Soldiers Blue and Gray* (Columbia: University of South Carolina Press, 1988); and Gerald F. Linderman, *Embattled Courage: The Experience*

*of Combat in the American Civil War* (New York and London: Free Press, 1987).

23. Diary entry, February 27, 1864.

24. Ibid., August 31, 1864.

25. Ibid., April 10, 1864.

26. Ibid., August 31, and October 8, 1864.

27. Ibid., April 18, 1864.

28. Ibid., March 13, 1864.

29. Ibid., March 18, 1864.

30. Letter from Captain Thomas M. Brunson to Captain [William E.] Yancey, January 22, 1865. Rainwater Collection.

31. Diary entry, March 19, 1865.

32. William Best Hesseltine, *Civil War Prisons: A Study in War Psychology* (New York: Frederick Ungar Publishing Co., 1964).

33. Diary entry, April 26, 1865.

34. See diary entries under the heading, "Sayings of Madam Rumor," April 10–June 6, 1865.

35. Ibid., April 16, 1865.

36. Ibid., June 6, 1865.

37. Undated theater advertisements for October 1866, in Williams Scrapbooks. Rainwater Collection.

38. *Cocoa* [Florida] *Tribune*, November 24, 1921. See C. A. Rohrabacher, *Live Towns and Progressive Men of Florida* (Jacksonville: Times-Union Printing and Publishing House, 1887), 184–85. See also undated advertisements in Williams Scrapbooks. Rainwater Collection. Williams had two children, Edmund Sidney and Myra Gray.

39. John Hardy, *Selma: Her Institutions and Her Men* (Spartanburg: Reprint Co., Publishers, 1978), 54. See undated advertisements in Williams Scrapbooks. Rainwater Collection.

40. Rohrabacher, *Live Towns*, 184.

41. School Board appointment letter, April 13, 1880, and Executive Department appointment certificate, April 23, 1881, Rainwater Collection.

42. Rohrabacher, *Live Towns*, 185. See also *Cocoa* [Florida] *Tribune*, November 24, 1921.

## 1. From Mobile to Dalton

1. Proprietor of Walker's Book Store, 102 Dauphin Street, Mobile, Alabama. Apparently, Mary Jane Walker was a family friend from New Jersey, since HSW's brother asked him to "Tell Mary I saw her sister to-day, well and doing well." Published letter, E. W. to H.S.W., December 18, 1863. Undated newspaper clipping, Williams Scrapbook, Rainwater Collection. See Census of 1860, Mobile.

2. Williams' opposition to reporting to Dalton was slightly more than moderate. See petition for transfer into the Confederate Navy, dated February 10, 1864. Photocopy in Editor's possession. See also Joseph E. Johnston, *Narrative of Military Operations Directed During the Late War Between the States* (Bloomington: Indiana University Press, 1959), 280, and James F. Clanahan, *The History of Pickens County, Alabama 1540–1920* (Carrollton, Ala.: Clanahan Publications, n.d.), 99–100. For an assessment of the ability of General Joseph E. Johnston to appeal to the common soldier, see Sprott, "Sumter," who writes, "Gen. Johnston was the beau ideal of a soldier, and his very appearance won for him the love and confidence of his soldier."

3. Blakely, Alabama, was the county seat of Baldwin County from 1820 to 1868. It served as a major transportation hub connecting the water traffic from Mobile Bay with the Mobile and Great Northern Railroad. From this point, cargo and passengers could link up with other railroads leading to the Upper South. See Robert C. Black III, *The Railroads of the Confederacy* (Chapel Hill: University of North Carolina Press, 1952), 6.

4. Mrs. David G. Brandt of 132 State Street, Mobile. The Census of 1860 and 1870 lists a grocery store at the corner of Law and State Streets belonging to David G. Brandt. It is likely that HSW boarded with the Brandts during his detached military service in Mobile. A grocer's wife certainly would have access to the delicacies mentioned by HSW.

5. Theodore Hamilton managed the Montgomery theater. *Caesar de Bazan* was a popular play of the period. In all probability, Williams had been a member of the cast when it was produced in Mobile in December 1863. See Mobile *Advertiser and Register,* December 2, 1863.

6. Cecelia Crisp was a member of a touring family of actors headed

by William H. Crisp and his wife, Jessie. See Letter to the Editor, Mobile *Advertiser and Register*, October 4, 1862.

7. Charles Morton was an actor and the co-manager of the Montgomery theater. See Montgomery *Daily Advertiser*, February 24, 1864.

8. The 40th Alabama had been a part of the Tennessee campaign under General Braxton E. Bragg, fighting at Chickamauga, Lookout Mountain, and Missionary Ridge. Following the end of that campaign, the regiment wintered in Dalton and few soldiers were given leave. News from home was a particularly scarce commodity, so fresh-from-home Williams was a welcome source of news. Evans, *Confederate Military History*, VII, 180–83.

9. Joshua J. Aughe, a musician, was wounded, captured, and paroled at Vicksburg. See Vicksburg Parole List, Vicksburg National Park; and Sprott, "Sumter," 19. J. A. Springsteed is listed on the March 15, 1862, muster roll for Company C, and mentioned by last name in Sprott. The circumstances surrounding his departure are unknown. F. M. Bradley was wounded at Vicksburg, but was later called back into the service. He surrendered at Mobile on April 12, 1865. See Muster Roll, Company C, 40th Alabama Infantry Regiment and Alabama Pension Record, Number 38316, State of Alabama Department of Archives and History. Hereafter referred to as ADAH.

10. The 40th Alabama participated in a number of the Mississippi campaigns. See Evans, *Confederate Military History*, VII, 180–83. See also, "History of Company 'B' 40th Alabama Regiment Originally 'Pickens Planters'" in Clanahan, *Pickens County*, 51–122.

11. A notation appears at the bottom of this page in the original diary: "cannot say how H. C. Harris is killed, June 8th, 63." Contrary to Williams' note, H. C. Harris was very much alive. He was fatally wounded in the shoulder and breast on May 14, 1864, while "skirmishing at Resaca, Ga." Pension Petition Records, ADAH. Also see, Sprott, "Sumter," 7.

12. Jones gave up his company command and served as an engineer on the staff of General Alexander Peter Stewart, a division, and later corps, commander in the Army of Tennessee. After the war, Jones achieved prominence as an engineer and a politician in Alabama. See Thomas M. Owen, *History of Alabama and Dictionary of Alabama Biography* (Spartanburg: Reprint Co., 1978), III, 943–44.

13. Thomas M. Brunson was listed as a 2nd Lieutenant on the

March 15, 1862, Muster Roll of Company C. ADAH. He assumed regimental command in March 1865 as the Army of Tennessee fought its last battles in North Carolina. Evans, *Confederate Military History,* VII, 183.

14. Stanley F. Horn describes the choice of Dalton for winter quarters as having "not been dictated by any military factors; it was simply the place where the army had stopped to rest when it retreated from Missionary Ridge and where Bragg left it when he resigned from command." Stanley F. Horn, *The Army of Tennessee: A Military History* (Indianapolis and New York: Bobbs-Merrill Co., 1941), 311.

15. The actual strength of the Army of Tennessee in February 1864 is hard to determine. General estimates put its numbers at between 35,000 and 45,000 effectives. See Robert M. Hughes, *General Johnston* (New York: D. Appleton and Co., 1897), 224–25.

16. For an interesting look at the quality and quantity of foodstuffs available to the Army of Tennessee, see Robert A. Taylor, "Rebel Beef: Florida Cattle and the Confederate Army, 1862–1864," *Florida Historical Quarterly* 67 (July 1988), 15–31.

17. Clanahan, *Pickens County,* 99.

18. Lieutenant John T. Terry, Company B, 40th Alabama Infantry Regiment. See Muster Roll, March 24, 1862. ADAH.

19. See unpublished diary, "Time Wears Wearily On," of Thomas P. Davis, Company H, 80th Illinois Volunteers, entry for February 25, 1864. Typescript in Special Collections Department, University of South Florida Library. This unsuccessful movement against the Confederate position at Dalton was led by General George H. Thomas. See Horn, *Army,* 316.

20. See Horn, *Army,* 316.

21. Ibid. According to Horn, General John Bell Hood joined the Army of Tennessee at this critical juncture "embued with the enthusiasm for a forward movement which he had absorbed from [Jefferson] Davis, [Braxton E.] Bragg and [Robert E.] Lee."

22. Ibid.

23. The pen name of Samuel Butler (1612–1680), an English satirist who commented on the follies of the courts and nobility of Europe.

24. Ezra J. Warner, *Generals in Gray: Lives of Confederate Commanders* (Baton Rouge: Louisiana State University Press, 1959), 52–53.

25. Entry dated February 27, 1864, in Davis, "Time," 72.

26. For a look at the role played by the 85th Illinois in the Atlanta Campaign, see Frederick H. Dyer, *A Compendium of the War of the Rebellion* (New York and London: Thomas Yoseloff, 1959), III, 1081–83.

27. See Taylor, "Rebel Beef," 15–31.

28. Oliver, a member of the 44th Tennessee Regiment, won high praise for his skillful use of the Pioneers Corps attached to General Alexander P. Stewart's Division during the Atlanta Campaign. See "Report of Major General Alexander P. Stewart, C.S. Army, Commanding Division, of Operations May 7–27 [1864]," in Bromfield L. Ridley, *Battle Sketches of the Army of Tennessee* (Mexico, Missouri: Missouri Printing and Publishing Co., 1906), 306–07. The organization of Pioneer units was mandated by the Confederate Congress in December 1863 at the division level. Although neither General Bragg nor General Johnston created such groups for the Army of Tennessee, apparently some divisional commanders like Stewart did obey the congressional mandate. See Jeffrey N. Lash, *Destroyer of the Iron Horse: General Joseph E. Johnston and Confederate Rail Transportation, 1861–1865* (Kent: Kent State University Press, 1991), 133.

29. The ability of members of the Pioneer Corps to move from one position to another and their close association with headquarters and hospital groups provided them with the opportunity to secure the best forage for themselves.

30. See "General W. T. Sherman's Report of the Dalton-Atlanta Campaign" in Ridley, *Battle Sketches,* 368. Sherman notes the tactical importance of these dams, which flooded the roads between Dalton and Tunnel Hill and which made it necessary to flank the Confederate lines by moving south to Snake Creek Gap.

31. "Mack" is probably William McMullen, a constant companion of Williams during his duty in the Pioneers. "Duncan" is not identifiable, for members of the Pioneers were drawn from various regiments in a division and were carried on the rolls of their original units.

32. Entry dated March 22, 1864, in Davis, "Time," 75.

33. Ridley, *Battle Sketches,* 368.

34. For a fuller examination of the outbreak of religiosity among Confederate troops in 1864–65, see Bell I. Wiley, *The Life of Johnny Reb* (Indianapolis and New York: Bobbs-Merrill Co., 1943), 174–91,

or James I. Robertson, Jr., *Soldiers Blue and Gray* (Columbia: University of South Carolina Press, 1988), 170–89. See also Herman Norton, *Rebel Religion: The Story of Confederate Chaplains* (St. Louis: Bethany Press, 1961). Sprott, "Sumter," 65, describes the revival movement as without "undue excitement, and nothing done or said—as is sometimes the case upon revival occasions, for effect, but every thing was calmly and deliberately done by serious men intent on serious business. This revival was not confined to our brigade or division but pervaded the entire army."

35. Richard M. McMurry, *John Bell Hood and the War for Southern Independence* (Lexington: University Press of Kentucky, 1982), 99–100.

36. Wiley, *Johnny Reb*, 174–91.

37. Many Southerners agreed with Williams' biting assessment of Jefferson Davis. For a critical assessment of Davis' role as commander-in-chief of the Confederate Army, see Clement Eaton, *Jefferson Davis* (New York: Free Press, 1977).

38. Mary Elizabeth Braddon (1835–1915) was a controversial English author and actress; her unconventional alliances with married men made her novels, plays, and volumes of poetry best sellers. She, along with her husband, John Maxwell, edited several magazines. Her stage name was Mary Seyton, and she also published under the pseudonyms, "Babington White" and "Aunt Belinda." *Aurora Floyd* was published in London in 1863. The fact that Williams was able to secure a copy so quickly after its initial printing is a testimony to the efficiency of blockade runners even as late as 1864.

39. Private Lucius Potter was a member of Company C, 36th Alabama Infantry Regiment. Pension application dated June 9, 1899, ADAH.

40. See undated printed letter, E. W. to H. S. W., Mobile *Advertiser and Register*, December 18, 1863. Williams apparently received a handwritten note from his brother, Edmund, that said essentially the same things as the printed version.

41. Ibid.

42. This is most likely Dr. George J. Colgin, a Sumter County physician, who was appointed as surgeon to the 40th Alabama in May 1862. Sprott, "Sumter," 6. For a more in-depth look at the Confederate medical service, see Horace H. Cunningham, *Doctors in Gray: The*

*Confederate Medical Service* (Baton Rouge: Louisiana State University Press, 1958), 284–85.

43. See undated advertising circular for "Kittatinny Blackberry . . . introduced by E. Williams, Montclair, N.J." Williams Scrapbook, Rainwater Collection.

44. McMurry, *Hood*, 98–100.

45. Clanahan, *Pickens County*, 100.

46. This demonstration, on April 29, was in preparation for the beginning of General W. T. Sherman's campaign against the Army of Tennessee, which was scheduled to start on May 5.

## 2. Prologue of the Great Battle

1. William Tecumseh Sherman, *Memoirs of General W. T. Sherman* (New York: Literary Classics of the United States, 1990), 494–96. The actual date of the start of the Georgia Campaign changed from April 30, to May 5, and then to May 7, in order to allow all the Union components to get into place for a simultaneous advance against the Army of Tennessee.

2. W. C. Dodson, ed., *Campaigns of Wheeler and His Cavalry, 1862–1865* (Atlanta: Hudgins Publishing Co., 1899), 175. See also, Johnston, *Narrative,* 305.

3. For a look at the role played by artillery in the Army of Tennessee during the Atlanta Campaign, see Larry J. Daniel, *Cannoneers in Gray: The Field Artillery of the Army of Tennessee, 1861–1865* (Tuscaloosa and London: University of Alabama Press, 1984), 143–66.

4. Sprott, "Sumter," 70–71. Sprott describes the dead soldier as "a young boy belonging to Co. C, whose name I cannot now recall, who had only been with us a few weeks." See also, Davis, "Time," 81–82.

5. Davis, "Time," 81–82.

6. Daniel, *Cannoneers,* 143–44; Davis, "Time," 82; and Johnston, *Narrative,* 306–08.

7. Johnston, *Narrative,* 307.

8. Davis, "Time," 82; Sprott, "Sumter," 71; and Daniel, *Cannoneers,* 143.

9. Formerly known as McCants' Florida Battery. Captain Robert P. McCants was arrested for habitual drunkenness and, in order to avoid

a court martial, he resigned. The battery was then placed under the command of Lieutenant Thomas J. Perry. Daniel, *Cannoneers,* 140.

10. Ridley, *Battle Sketches,* 306–07.

11. Davis, "Time," 82.

12. Sprott, "Sumter," 71.

13. Davis, "Time," 82.

14. Williams was skeptical of rumors of overwhelming Confederate successes during this period. In many ways, this is a reflection of his increasingly anti-military authority attitude.

15. Sprott, "Sumter," 71.

16. See Davis, "Time," 82. The entry for May 11, 1864, closely follows Williams' remarks, "This morning is dark and rainy. Last night wee had a powerful hard rain. I got verry wet. It come through the top and run under me and at the same time I could [not] sleep."

17. Sprott, "Sumter," 71; Evans, *Confederate Military History,* VII, 180–83; and Clanahan, *Pickens County,* 101.

18. Davis, "Time," 82; Dodson, *Wheeler,* 177–78; Johnston, *Narrative,* 308–09; and McMurry, *Hood,* 102.

19. Williams is referring to Sugar Valley, "on the Resaca side of Snake-Creek Gap." Sherman, *Memoirs,* 500–01.

20. Ibid.; and Johnston, *Narrative,* 308–09.

21. The Connesauga or Connasauga River. Tilton was the location of Hood's Corps, which protected Johnston's right flank. Tilton was the scene of major fighting on May 12–13. See McMurry, *Hood,* 103–06.

22. Sprott, "Sumter," 72–74.

23. Dodson, *Wheeler,* 177–78; and Daniel, *Cannoneers,* 144–45.

24. Oostenaula River.

25. Sherman, *Memoirs,* 503. See also Johnston, *Narrative,* 312–14.

26. McMurry, *Hood,* 103–06.

## 3. The Great Battle

1. George W. Pepper, *Personal Recollections of Sherman's Campaigns in Georgia and the Carolinas* (Zanesville, Ohio: Hugh Dunne, 1866), 62–64; and Sherman, *Memoirs,* 500–03.

2. Cunningham, *Doctors in Gray,* 117–22, provides a graphic de-

scription of the operation of field hospitals. For another view by an officer attached to Sherman's army, see Pepper, *Recollections*, 158–62.

3. Linderman, *Embattled Courage*, 28–31, 130–33.

4. Sprott, "Sumter," 73–74. See also, Horn, *Army*, 325. The attack of late afternoon, May 14, was by Hood's corps. The next morning, Hood's forces were attacked by Federal units under the command of General Joseph Hooker.

5. Sprott, "Sumter," 7. See note 11, Chapter 1.

6. Williams was worried, apparently, that he might be killed and buried in an unknown grave. He mentions this possibility several times throughout his diary. For similar sentiments, see Robertson, *Soldiers Blue and Gray*, 224–28.

7. Sprott, "Sumter," 72; Dodson, *Wheeler*, 179; and Johnston, *Narrative*, 312.

8. Sherman, *Memoirs*, 503; and Davis, "Time," 83.

9. Daniel, *Cannoneers*, 145; Sherman, *Memoirs*, 503–06; and Johnston, *Narrative*, 312–14.

10. Pepper, *Recollections*, 158–62. See also Lloyd Lewis, *Sherman: Fighting Prophet* (New York: Harcourt, Brace and Co., 1958), 364–65.

11. Davis, "Time," 85; Sherman, *Memoirs*, 504; Sprott, "Sumter," 75; and Johnston, *Narrative*, 312–14.

12. Johnston, *Narrative*, 314.

13. Ibid.

14. Ibid. See also Sherman, *Memoirs*, 504–11; McMurry, *Hood*, 106–08.

15. Ibid.

16. Thomas P. Davis noted in his diary on the same date, "This is verry nice country through here, thare is a general destruction of property whaer wee gow." Davis, "Time," 84.

17. Ibid. On May 20, Davis noted the destruction wrought by both the Union and Confederate soldiers, "This is a verry rugged and nice place, but the soldiers has toar it up terribly. Some of the refugees are coming back this morning to find their houses ransacked and everything taken out."

18. Ibid. Staying in Cassville several days as his unit rested, Davis noted, "The people here are wanting peace again, they see their folly now when it is too late."

19. McMurry, *Hood,* 108–09.

20. Ibid. Johnston ignored the advice of his Chief of Artillery, General Francis A. Shoup, who had warned that his position was subject to being enfiladed by Sherman's cannon.

21. Confederate generals Johnston, Polk, and Hood met at Polk's headquarters to discuss the situation. Despite Hood's assertion that he and Polk wanted to use the Cassville position for offensive, rather than defensive, purposes, Johnston decided to retreat. Ibid. Johnston later maintained that his line at Cassville was "the best that I saw occupied during the war." His postwar contention was that he decided to evacuate Cassville "in the belief that the confidence of the commanders of two of the three corps of the army, of their inability to resist the enemy, would inevitably be communicated to their troops, and produce that inability." This conflict at Cassville was part of the developing feud between Hood and Johnston. Johnston, *Narrative,* 321–24. See also Sherman, *Memoirs,* 507–11.

22. Lewis, *Sherman,* 361. Lewis quotes part of Johnston's order, "You will now turn and march to meet his advancing columns. . . . I lead you to battle."

23. Ibid. See also Daniel, *Cannoneers,* 147; and Sprott, "Sumter," 76.

24. Clanahan, *Pickens County,* 102.

25. So quickly was the Army of Tennessee falling back from position to position that the supply wagons could not keep up with the retreat. It was not only a Confederate problem, but a Union one as well. Supplies that had been carefully collected and husbanded were left behind as units moved quickly.

26. Williams is referring to his years of traveling in the Midwest as a supporter of Millard Fillmore in 1856 and as an adventurer in 1857–58. See original diaries for these years in Rainwater Collection.

27. Most likely Nancy Creek.

28. See Sprott, "Sumter," 76. Sprott describes the biscuits as "thick pones, and after the second day would be filled with mould that when it was broken it looked like it was filled with spider web."

29. Johnston's forces paused for almost two days following the evacuation of Cassville and camped on the east side of the Etowah River. Clanahan, *Pickens County,* 102.

30. Probably Pickett's Mill and Foundry. See map, Sherman,

*Memoirs,* 509–13. Although Johnston wanted to confront Sherman on favorable terrain at Allatoona Pass, Sherman, who had surveyed the area during an assignment to Marietta in 1844, refused to engage him. Instead, he directed his forces to flank Johnston by moving west to Dallas.

31. Davis, "Time," 85. Davis' opinion of the land around Allatoona coincided with Williams'. It was, he wrote, "ruff country" and "verry hilly."

32. Most probably Pumpkin Vine Creek. Sherman, *Memoirs,* 509.

33. Davis, "Time," 85.

34. Clanahan, *Pickens County,* 102; Sprott, "Sumter," 77–83; Johnston, *Narrative,* 326–35; and Sherman, *Memoirs,* 513–15.

35. Daniel, *Cannoneers,* 148–50. The Battle of New Hope Church produced approximately 1,500 Union casualties and about 500 for the Confederates. The tremendous firing of small arms and artillery cut swaths through forests. Men on both sides of the battle called the area around New Hope Church the "Hell Hole." McMurry, *Hood,* 110–11. Sherman, however, referred to this battle as "the drawn battle of New Hope Church." Sherman, *Memoirs,* 518. Sprott, "Sumter," p. 83, places the number of Union soldiers killed at "five or six thousand, killed or wounded."

36. Clanahan, *Pickens County,* 103, states that "Many killed and wounded in the 40th."

37. Sherman, *Memoirs,* 513–14. These flanking movements were conducted by General George H. Thomas and John M. Schofield, two corps commanders in Sherman's army.

38. Sprott, "Sumter," 82–83, recounts a rather bizarre story about Private R. J. McGowen of the 37th Alabama, who was stunned by the concussion of a shell and came within seconds of being buried alive. "As they took him up to roll him in his blanket preparatory to laying him in his grave, he gave a kick, and he was laid down and in a few minutes was able to sit up. . . . A few minutes more to the horror of war would have been added that of being buried alive."

39. Ridley, *Battle Sketches,* 308, quotes General Stewart's report, which noted that "Baker's and Clayton's men had piled up a few logs and Stovall's Georgians were without any defense." See also, Johnston, *Narrative,* 328.

40. Sherman, *Memoirs,* 514.

41. Daniel, *Cannoneers*, 149–50. See also James M. McPherson, *Ordeal By Fire: The Civil War and Reconstruction* (New York: Alfred A. Knopf, 1982), 288–91.

42. Daniel, *Cannoneers*, 149–50.

43. Sprott, "Sumter," 83.

44. Johnston, *Narrative*, 333–34. This movement was a prelude to a planned attack by Hood's Corps. When Hood unexpectedly encountered Union forces in positions he had not anticipated, he delayed attacking. Johnston subsequently called off the planned assault. This episode became another in a long list of disputes between Hood and Johnston.

45. Ibid. The failure of Hood to carry out the planned assault ended the fighting around New Hope Church. Johnston was forced to move his forces continuously to interpose them between the Union army and the Western and Atlantic Railroad.

46. McMurry, *Hood*, 111. For the rest of May, both sides participated in limited infantry skirmishes. Major General Joseph Wheeler, Johnston's cavalry commander, carried out several minor attacks on Federal positions. See also Dodson, *Wheeler*, 188–89.

47. This drama was written in 1839 by Edward George Earle Lytton, Lord Bulwer-Lytton (1803–1873) and originally was titled *Richelieu; or The Conspiracy*. Laurie Lanzen Harris, ed., *Nineteenth-Century Literature Criticism* (Detroit: Gale Research Co., 1981), 134.

48. Arthur W. Bergeron, Jr., *Guide to Louisiana Confederate Military Units, 1861–1865* (Baton Rouge and London: Louisiana State University Press, 1989), 120.

49. Johnston, *Narrative*, 335. Following the Battle of New Hope Church, Sherman continuously spread his forces to try to flank Johnston. In preparation for a withdrawal to prevent his army's encirclement, Johnston had his Chief of Engineers, Colonel S. W. Prestman, prepare defensive positions in advance of such moves.

50. Ibid.

51. Clanahan, *Pickens County*, 104.

52. Johnston, *Narrative*, 336. Williams' assessment was correct. The Union army moved eastward toward the Western and Atlantic Railroad and centered its forces at Pine Mountain in Cobb County.

53. Johnston, *Narrative*, 337; McMurry, *Hood*, 111; and Sherman, *Memoirs*, 523–25. It is interesting that Sherman felt compelled to

defend himself against the allegation that he "fired the gun which killed General Polk," to which he responded, "I was on horseback, a couple of hundred yards off, before my orders to fire were executed."

54. The 40th Alabama became involved in an effort to stem a break in the Confederate lines along Noonday Creek by Union forces belonging to General O. O. Howard. Howard claimed to have captured all of the 40th Alabama, a claim hotly disputed by survivors. Sprott, "Sumter," 87–89. Clanahan, *Pickens County*, 105–06, places the losses at 146 enlisted men and 9 officers.

55. Big Shanty served as the principal supply depot for Sherman's forces operating around Kennesaw Mountain. The Western and Atlantic Railroad, destroyed during Johnston's retreat, was repaired, and supply trains could deliver matériel directly to Big Shanty. Each Union division sent wagons to Big Shanty to procure supplies. Sherman, *Memoirs*, 520.

56. McMurry, *Hood*, 112; Daniel, *Cannoneers*, 151; and Sherman, *Memoirs*, 525–26. Sherman was so impressed with the Confederate defenses and their utility that he authorized the creation of a Union Pioneer Corps of contrabands who had escaped to Union lines. They were to be paid $10 a month.

57. Sherman, *Memoirs*, 525.

58. Johnston, *Narrative*, 338–39; McMurry, *Hood*, 112; and Pepper, *Recollections*, 81–82.

59. Sprott, "Sumter," 89.

60. Clanahan, *Pickens County*, 106–07.

61. Sprott, "Sumter," 90–91, provides another description of this action.

## 4. Atlanta

1. Pepper, *Recollections*, 90.

2. This bridge probably spanned Noyes [Nose] Creek.

3. Lieutenant James W. Monett. Muster Roll, Company C, 40th Alabama Regiment, ADAH. See also, Sprott, "Sumter," 8.

4. General John Bell Hood responded to an attempt to outflank the Confederate position on Kenesaw Mountain by the Union Army of the Ohio by conducting an unauthorized attack on the advancing Federals

at Kolb's Farm. The rebels' repeated charges were halted at the cost of about 1,000 casualties. General John M. Schofield's Army of the Ohio lost less than 300 men. See Jacob D. Cox, *Atlanta* (New York: Charles Scribner and Sons, 1882), 110–13. See also Johnston, *Narrative*, 340.

5. Cox, *Atlanta*, 116–17. Following Hood's defeat at Kolb's Farm, Sherman nevertheless decided to pull back Schofield's division, which was engaged in a flanking movement along Sandtown Road. Sherman's decision was based on intelligence that Johnston had been reinforced by a full division of Georgia militia under General G. W. Smith.

6. The Hamilton family resided a short distance south of the Powder Springs Road.

7. A frustrated Sherman hurled his troops against the strongly held Kennesaw Mountain in a poorly planned assault on June 27th. All three Union attacks failed, and those regiments engaged suffered heavy losses. General Benjamin F. Cheatham's Confederate division had been charged by elements of Union General John M. Palmer's 14th Corps, which likewise were bloodied. By the time the attack was called off at 11:30 A.M., Sherman had lost from 2,000 to 3,000 casualties, while Confederate losses were around 500. Sherman referred to the action as "the hardest fight of the campaign to that date." Sherman, *Memoirs*, 531; Cox, *Atlanta*, 127; and Horn, *Army*, 336–37.

8. This stream was most probably Nickajack Creek. Johnston had prepared another defensive line along its banks. See Horn, *Army*, 338; and E. B. Long, *The Civil War Day By Day: An Almanac 1861–1865* (Garden City: Doubleday, 1971), 532.

9. On July 4th, Sherman directed General James McPherson's Army of the Tennessee to attempt to turn the Confederate left flank and push for the Chattahoochee River. Hood's Confederate corps was unable to stop this advance, and Johnston was forced to make another limited withdrawal. Johnston, *Narrative*, 346; and Sherman, *Memoirs*, 535–36.

10. Chattahoochee River.

11. Stewart actually took command of Polk's old corps, temporarily under General William Wing Loring, on July 7, 1864. Johnston, *Narrative*, 347.

12. The Confederate line north of the Chattahoochee ran roughly from the Western and Atlantic Railroad bridge to Turner's Ferry on the left. Williams was correct about the scarcity of Confederate artillery

fire. Because of a shortage of ammunition, batteries only fired to repel attacks or during actual battle. Ibid., 346. See also, Thomas L. Connelly, *Autumn of Glory: The Army of Tennessee 1862–1865* (Baton Rouge: Louisiana State University Press, 1971), 364.

13. McPherson's Army of the Tennessee was demonstrating in the Turner's Ferry area to draw attention away from a Union thrust across the Chattahoochee at the mouth of Soap Creek on the Confederate right by General Schofield's troops. Long, *Almanac*, 535. See also Sherman, *Memoirs*, 540–42.

14. Each corps of Johnston's army was assigned two bridges for the retreat across the Chattahoochee. Confederate artillery rolled across first, followed by the infantry around 10:00 P.M. on July 9th. After the rearguard was safely on the southern bank at 1:00 A.M., the pontoon bridges were taken up and the fixed bridges burned. Cox, *Atlanta*, 141; Johnston, *Narrative*, 346–47; and Sherman, *Memoirs*, 542.

15. Snake Creek Gap outside Dalton.

16. Sprott, "Sumter," 93–94. Sprott records a very angry reaction by members of the 40th Alabama to Johnston's removal, citing Sherman, who supposedly said, ". . . the removal of Gen[eral] Johnston was worth a reinforcement of 10,000 men to his army." He maintains that "the officers and men had the most unbounded love for, and confidence in, General Johnston. So great was it that had one regiment or brigade stacked arms and refused to fight under General Hood, almost the entire army would have done likewise."

17. For another view of the reaction of the Army of Tennessee to this change in command, see Connelly, *Autumn*, 423.

18. Thomas' Union Army of the Cumberland drove Confederate pickets back across Peachtree Creek and by noon, July 19, had begun crossing it in force. See Sherman, *Memoirs*, 544; Connelly, *Autumn*, 439; and John B. Hood, *Advance and Retreat* (New Orleans: Hood Orphan Memorial Fund, 1880), 166.

19. Lewis, *Sherman*, 383. Lewis mentions the blackberry patch as an attraction that spoiled Hood's surprise attack at Peachtree Creek, to wit, "Private Henry E. Cist, Company I, Twenty-third Indiana, stood on his trench looking at blackberries just beyond the skirmishers. He had been awaiting battle for three days, and was tired of it. He wanted those blackberries, and as the quiet of noon descended he stole out to them. He rambled nearer the forest, picking and eating. Suddenly a

flash of light dazzled his eyes. He blinked. It was the sun striking on gun barrels of gray-coated men pouring out of the forest—six lines of them, muskets at right-shoulder shift. Cist screamed murder, Rebels, help, get ready, and bounded homeward through the briers, berry stains on his open lips. His comrades dropped their noonday meals, cannon boomed, musket volleys crashed—and the fight was on." See also Sherman, *Memoirs*, 544–48.

20. Hood ordered an attack against Thomas' isolated army in what was known as the Battle of Peachtree Creek. Confusion, tardiness, and poor execution of plan marked Hood's debut as commander of the Army of Tennessee. Hood would later try to blame General William J. Hardee, a competitor for command of the army, for the disaster. During the two-hour battle, the Confederates suffered 4,800 casualties, while Union losses were 1,780. See Paul M. Angle, ed., *Three Years in the Army of the Cumberland: The Letters and Diary of Major James A. Connolly* (Bloomington: Indiana University Press, 1959), 239; Connelly, *Autumn*, 441; Long, *Almanac*, 542; and Sherman, *Memoirs*, 547.

21. Pepper, *Recollections*, 104. Pepper notes, "The greater portion of the inhabitants of Atlanta have, in conformity with the orders and warnings of rebel commanders, abandoned their houses and homes and gone—God only knows where."

22. Hardee's Corps was once again thrown against Sherman on July 22 in the Battle of Atlanta. An attempt to turn the Union flank cost Hood between 7,000 and 8,000 men. Sherman's losses were put at 3,722. The most notable casualty of this fighting was General James B. McPherson. Hood looked for scapegoats for his failure and blamed his soldiers for a lack of aggressiveness brought on by the "timid defensive" policies of his predecessor, Johnston. See Hood, *Advance*, 183; Cox, *Atlanta*, 176; and Long, *Almanac*, 544.

23. The Army of the Tennessee, now under the command of General O. O. Howard, began a march around Atlanta south of the Chattahoochee to seal off the city's links with the rest of the Confederacy. See Hood, *Advance*, 193; and Sherman, *Memoirs*, 560.

24. The Battle of Ezra Church was the third and final attempt by Hood to defeat Sherman by taking the offensive. This battle produced approximately 5,000 casualties for Hood, compared to approximately 600 for Sherman. See Cox, *Atlanta*, 185; Sherman, *Memoirs*, 563–65;

and Long, *Almanac,* 547. Major Connolly summed up his opinion about the Confederate's tactics at Ezra Church, "It was perfect murder. We slaughter them by the thousands, but Hood continues to hurl his broken, bleeding battalions against our immoveable lines with all the fury of a maniac. Reason seems dethroned." Angle, *Three Years,* 247.

25. Sprott, "Sumter," 94–96.

26. Union forces were prevented from cutting the Atlanta and West Point Railroad in the Battle of Utoy Church. See Albert Castel, "Union Fizzle at Atlanta: The Battle of Utoy Church," *Civil War Times Illustrated,* Vol. 16, No. 10 (February 1978): 26–32.

27. On August 19, Pioneer detachments were ordered to block all roads leading from Camp Creek Church toward East Point and to construct fortifications closer to Union lines. *O. R.,* Series 1, Vol. 48, Part 5, 967, 976.

28. Lewis, *Sherman,* 371. Lewis provides an excellent description of these devices, which were called sheep racks by Union soldiers.

29. Sherman, *Memoirs,* 578. This cannonading was a cover for Sherman's next move, which was to pull troops from the line and begin a full encirclement of Atlanta.

30. Ibid. Sherman withdrew the 20th Corps on the night of the 25th and the 15th and 17th Corps on the 26th. He noted in his *Memoirs* that "the enemy did not detect the change at all." The stratagem worked so well that almost everyone believed the Union armies had withdrawn. So convinced were the Confederates, he writes, that "several trains of cars (with ladies) came up from Macon to assist in the celebration of their grand victory."

31. Cox, *Atlanta,* 197–98; and Dodson, *Wheeler,* 248–51. This abundance of foodstuffs in deserted Union positions belied Hood's belief that General Joseph Wheeler's cavalry, which had gone North on August 10 to attack the railroad between Chattanooga and Marietta, was successful in so destroying Sherman's supply lines that he was forced to retreat from Atlanta.

32. Sprott, "Sumter," 95–96. Although the 40th Alabama had been transferred to Mobile on August 6, Williams was not included in the transfer, for he was still detached to the Pioneer Corps.

33. Sherman, *Memoirs,* 579. On August 28, Sherman's forces severed the West Point Railroad. Sherman gave a vivid description of his hated "neckties" in his *Memoirs,* "The track was heaved up in sections

the length of a regiment, then separated rail by rail; bonfires were made of the ties and of fence-rails on which the rails were heated, carried to trees or telegraph poles, wrapped around and left to cool."

34. Sherman, *Memoirs,* 580–81. Hardee attempted to secure a victory over the Union 15th Corps, commanded by General James A. Logan, at Jonesboro, south of Atlanta. Rebel losses were approximately 1,725, while the Federals lost only 170 men killed or wounded.

35. Cox, *Atlanta,* 203–10. Hood, completely misreading Sherman's movements, recalled General Stephen D. Lee's corps from Jonesboro to Atlanta to defend against an attack that he felt was imminent. In the middle of Lee's march back to Atlanta, Hood changed his mind and directed him to go to Jonesboro once again. Only night saved Lee's divisions from complete destruction by Sherman, and only night allowed Hardee to break off his engagement with Logan. Hood's failure to read Sherman's activities cost him Atlanta, its factories, and matériel.

36. Sherman, *Memoirs,* 581–82; and Cox, *Atlanta,* 207–08. Sherman describes the sounds of Atlanta burning, "That night I was so restless and impatient that I could not sleep, and about midnight there arose toward Atlanta sounds of shells exploding, and other sounds like that of musketry. I walked to the house of a farmer close by my bivouac, called him out to listen to the reverberations which came from the direction of Atlanta (twenty miles north of us), and inquired of him if he had resided there long. He said he had, and that those sounds were just like those of a battle."

The decision to abandon Atlanta was particularly costly for Hood in terms of artillery ordnance—10 field pieces, 14 siege guns, 33 caissons, and, most important, the Army of Tennessee's entire reserve of artillery ammunition, 14,000 rounds. See Daniels, *Cannoneers,* 164–65.

## 5. Retreat from Atlanta

1. Davis, "Time," 103.

2. Sherman, *Memoirs,* 584. Sherman decided "not to attempt at that time a further pursuit of Hood's army, but slowly and deliberately to move back, occupy Atlanta, enjoy a short period of rest, and to think well over the next step required in the progress of events." Another

reason for Sherman's decision was the fact that almost one-third of his army was due for release in September as their terms of enlistment were completed. See Cox, *Atlanta*, 221.

3. Macon and Central Railroad. Hood was faced with a similar loss of manpower when Georgia Governor Joseph Emerson Brown withdrew the Georgia militia forces that had joined the Army of Tennessee for the siege of Atlanta. William Harris Bragg, *Joe Brown's Army: The Georgia State Line, 1862–1865* (Macon: Mercer University Press, 1987), 98–102. See also John P. Dyer, *The Gallant Hood* (Indianapolis and New York: Bobbs-Merrill Co., 1950), 273.

4. Lewis, *Sherman*, 422–34. Following the fall of Atlanta, Hood and the remaining 40,000 men of the Army of Tennessee sought to draw Sherman out of the city and northward by attacking the same positions along the Western and Atlantic Railroad that the Confederates had held just seven months earlier.

5. Sherman, *Memoirs*, 615–16. Sherman saw the movement of Hood's troops westward as an attempt to entice the Federal army to move into central Georgia and to continue to rely on an extended supply line that originated in Nashville. Sherman refused to accept this invitation to potential disaster.

6. Clement Eaton, *Jefferson Davis* (New York: Free Press, 1977), 255–56. Jefferson Davis, seeking to shore up Southern morale after Atlanta, visited Hood's headquarters at Palmetto on September 25. While there, he approved Hood's strategy to force Sherman to withdraw from Georgia by attacking his lines of supply.

7. Connelly, *Autumn*, 471; and Hood, *Advance*, 255. Following Davis' visit to Hood's headquarters, the order was given to move northward, and the Army of Tennessee crossed the Chattahoochee River at Pumpkin Town and Phillip's Ferry.

8. Cox, *Atlanta*, 225.

9. Ibid., 72–88.

10. On this march, General Stephen D. Lee, the corps commander, allowed each of his Pioneer units one tool wagon and one baggage wagon. *O. R.*, Series 1, Vol. 39, Part 3, 779, 805. Williams refers to Cedar Point, but most likely he means Cedartown. Sherman, *Memoirs*, 627.

11. Hood's plan was to turn from Cedartown to attack Rome, just a few miles from Cedartown, and then turn his forces toward the West-

ern and Atlantic at Kingston, but "he formed a more prudent plan, and crossing the Coosa about fifteen miles below Rome he followed the line of long valleys, protected by high rocky ridges, to Resaca." Cox, *Atlanta*, 234.

12. Sherman's frustration at playing catch-up to Hood and of having constantly to protect over 140 miles of railroad prompted him to write to General Ulysses S. Grant for permission to destroy the railroads between Chattanooga and Atlanta himself and to set off for Savannah. Sherman, *Memoirs*, 627.

13. Despite his misgivings about pursuing Hood, Sherman nevertheless sent troops after him. Davis, "Time," 107. On October 11, Hood, content with the game of cat-and-mouse, dispatched his wagons and reserve artillery to Jacksonville and Gadsden, Alabama, in order to keep his force as mobile as possible. Cox, *Atlanta*, 235.

14. The attack on small Union garrisons along the route of the Western and Atlantic Railroad was part of Hood's plan to force Sherman to abandon Atlanta and follow the Army of Tennessee northward. McPherson, *Ordeal*, 460.

15. Bragg, *Joe Brown's Army*, 94.

16. Cox, *Atlanta*, 237; and Sherman, *Memoirs*, 630. Sherman noted, "We found this gap very badly obstructed by fallen timber, but got through that night."

17. Sherman, *Memoirs*, 632. Although Sherman continued to pursue Hood, he was concentrating his energies on preparing for his bold march across Georgia to the sea.

18. Bragg, *Joe Brown's Army*, 94–95. Hood's retreat into Alabama created a crisis for part of his army. The Georgia militia, pursuant to the orders of Governor Joseph E. Brown, notified General Stephen D. Lee, to whose corps they were attached, that they would leave and go home. On October 21, when the Army of Tennessee reached Gadsden, the Georgia troops departed. At Gadsden, Hood was joined by General P. G. T. Beauregard, who assumed overall command of the Division of the West. Dyer, *Gallant Hood*, 273.

19. Ibid.

20. Johnston, *Narrative*, 167–68. For the story of Emma Sansom, see Lucille Griffith, *Alabama: A Documentary History to 1900* (University: University of Alabama Press, 1968), 398–405. The Federal army, encamped at Gaylesville, was at a critical point. Sherman, anx-

ious to begin his march through Georgia, decided to offer only token pursuit of Hood, and as he noted in his *Memoirs,* "At Gaylesville, the pursuit of Hood by the army under my immediate command may be said to have ceased."

21. Hood, *Advance,* 270. The Army of Tennessee's camp on October 22 was in the vicinity of Bennetsville.

22. Williams was actually crossing Racoon Mountain. Sand Mountain was a considerable distance to the northeast.

23. Sherman, *Memoirs,* 636. Hood moved his army to Decatur, Alabama. Sherman, seeking to satisfy himself that the Army of Tennessee was no threat to his troops in Georgia or his plan for a cross-state march, sent a reconnaissance to ascertain that Hood was on the move. Sherman was absolutely convinced that Hood would move into Tennessee and that Federal troops already there could handle the Confederates.

24. No reason for the arrest of Oliver and Grimley can be ascertained. Whatever the reason, Oliver, at least, did not suffer from it. He was a member of General A. P. Stewart's staff during the last campaign in the Carolinas. See Ridley, *Battle Sketches,* 468.

25. The Memphis and Charleston Railroad.

26. Horn, *Army,* 382. The bridge was finished on November 2, but heavy rains raised the level of the Tennessee River and partly submerged it. See also Dyer, *Gallant Hood,* 282–85.

27. Sprott, "Sumter," 95–96. The 40th Alabama had been transferred to Mobile on August 6.

28. Williams left the Army of Tennessee just as Hood was consolidating his forces for his invasion of Tennessee.

29. Hood, *Advance,* 382. A gap of ten miles existed in the railroad from Tuscumbia to Cherokee, and wagons were used in a relay to move supplies forward to Hood's army. In all probability, Williams caught a ride on one of these wagons.

30. McPherson, *Ordeal,* 292–93. On October 3–4, 1862, Union General William S. Rosecrans blocked efforts by Confederate Generals Earl Van Dorn and Sterling Price to join with General Braxton E. Bragg in Kentucky. Union casualties totaled 3,300, and Confederate casualties were approximately 5,700.

31. Probably Mrs. [Eliza P.] George W. Turner who operated a popular boardinghouse at the corner of St. Louis and Jackson streets.

## 6. From Mobile to Point Lookout Prison

1. For an account of the events around Mobile during this critical period, see John Kent Folmar, ed., *From That Terrible Field: Civil War Letters of James M. Williams, Twenty-first Alabama Infantry Volunteers* (University, Ala.: University of Alabama Press, 1981).

2. See Muster Roster, Company E, 40th Alabama Infantry Regiment, December 31, 1863, ADAH.

3. Muster Roll, Company C, 40th Alabama, ADAH.

4. Lash, *Destroyer,* 156. Lash gives the route of troops assemblying from the Army of Tennessee encampment at Tupelo and for troops coming from other points west.

5. Most probably the theatrical family of Charles Crisp. The title "captain" was probably an honorific. See reference to "Captain" Crisp in Mobile *Register and Advertiser,* December 6, 1863. Benson was a member of Company C, 40th Alabama. No first name or initials appear on the roster of that company in Sprott, "Sumter," 19.

6. A gap of twenty miles existed between Mayfield and Camak on the way to Augusta.

7. Remnants of the Army of Tennessee, which had been badly defeated in the Battles of Franklin and Nashville, were concentrating on crossing the Savannah River at Augusta for a temporary encampment at Aiken, South Carolina. John Bell Hood, who had been replaced by General Richard Taylor as commander of that group on January 18, was journeying toward Richmond and passed through Augusta at approximately the same time. McMurry, *Hood,* 183–85.

8. The cavalry of Union General Judson Kilpatrick and Confederate General Joseph E. Wheeler clashed at Aiken on February 11. Despite a victory by Wheeler, he was subsequently removed from command of the cavalry of the Army of Tennessee by General P. G. T. Beauregard. General Wade Hampton was placed in command of the cavalry forces. Following this encounter, Wheeler, Hampton, and the remainder of the army turned attention to the defense of Columbia. See John P. Dyer, *From Shiloh to San Juan: The Life of "Fightin' Joe" Wheeler* (Baton Rouge: Louisiana State University Press, 1961), 170–72.

9. On February 17, Union forces under Generals John A. Logan and Francis P. Blair entered Columbia and immediately began pillaging and destroying that city.

10. The lack of critical supplies made it necessary for the troops under Johnston's command to forage the countryside for food. Bradley T. Johnson, *A Memoir of the Life and Public Service of Joseph E. Johnston* (Baltimore: R. H. Woodward, 1891), 206.

11. Sprott, "Sumter," 102–03. Joseph E. Johnston, who had been languishing in exile following his removal from command of the Army of Tennessee before the Battle of Atlanta, was recalled to command the effort to stop Sherman from joining with Grant in the Carolinas. On February 23, Johnston received orders from General Robert E. Lee to undertake this task. Johnston, *Narrative*, 371.

12. Sprott, "Sumter," 20.

13. Johnson, *Life*, 207. Johnston selected Smithfield as the consolidation point for all troops under his command. On March 4, he established his headquarters at Fayetteville. Johnston anticipated that Sherman would try to cut the lines of supply to Lee's army by taking the railroad hub, Goldsboro.

14. Lash, *Destroyer*, 159–69. Johnston faced considerable problems transporting his troops to critical locations and constantly complained to General Robert E. Lee about the mismanagement of North Carolina railroads.

15. John G. Barrett, *Sherman's March Through the Carolinas* (Chapel Hill: University of North Carolina Press, 1956), 159–85.

16. Johnston, *Narrative*, 386–88.

17. Clanahan, *Pickens County*, 120–21.

18. Sherman, *Memoirs*, 787. Sherman placed his losses at Bentonville at 1,581 and Johnston's at 2,343.

19. Williams was probably captured by Union soldiers from either the 13th or 21st Michigan Infantry. Both were in the 2nd Brigade of the 1st Division and actively engaged at Bentonville. See *O. R.*, Series 1, Vol. 47, Part 1, 51.

20. Neuse River.

21. Point Lookout Prison was located on a peninsula formed by the Potomac River and the Chesapeake Bay in Maryland. Established originally as a Union army camp of instruction, by 1865 it was the largest prison camp for Confederates in the North. In April 1865, there were some 20,110 prisoners held in an enclosed space of some twenty acres. Housing consisted of tents that rumor had it were rejected for use by the Federal forces. Fresh water was in short supply, as were food

rations for the prisoners. These shortages combined with inadequate shelter caused a high level of sickness and death among the prison population. During the month of April, some 203 inmates died of disease. Complaints from Union medical officers about overcrowding at Point Lookout were all but ignored by Washington. For a look at conditions at Point Lookout, see Edwin B. Beitzell, *Point Lookout Prison Camp for Confederates* (Privately published, 1972). See also *Southern Historical Society Papers,* 52 Volumes (Richmond: Southern Historical Society, 1876–1959), 18: 116, 431–34 (hereafter cited as *SHSP*).

22. Rations for prisoners at Point Lookout were so scarce that Confederates were forced to supplement them with foodstuffs purchased from guards or the prison sutler. *SHSP,* 1: 258.

23. Officials at Point Lookout Prison followed a deliberate policy of not providing sufficient shelter for the Confederate prisoners there. This policy was apparently in retaliation for the treatment Union prisoners received at Andersonville Prison in Georgia and Libby Prison in Richmond. See Hesseltine, *Civil War Prisons.*

24. *SHSP,* Volume 1: 258.

## 7. Sayings of Madam Rumor

1. Edmund N. Hatcher, *The Last Four Weeks* (Columbus, Ohio: Edmund N. Hatcher, Publisher, 1891), 238–41.

2. Major Allen G. Brady became Provost Marshal in July 1864 after having served with the 17th Connecticut Infantry at Chancellorsville and Gettysburg. The majority of prisoners disliked Brady, who they thought stole money and other articles from their mail. He was sometimes referred to as "Brute" Brady. *SHSP,* 2: 237; 18: 23, 162.

3. Major Barnes was the Assistant Provost Marshal and the nephew of the camp's commander, General James Barnes. Unlike Brady, Barnes was considered kind and thoughtful by the Rebel prisoners. *SHSP,* 18: 422–33; and Beitzell, *Point Lookout,* 90.

4. Hatcher, *The Last Four Weeks,* 241–43.

5. Ibid., 272–74. Hatcher quotes officers of the Union army in Sherman's command as reacting bitterly to Lincoln's assassination. "Others with clinched fist and firm set teeth were calling for vengeance

upon the whole race of traitors, from Jeff[erson] Davis down. A people who could conceive of such transcendent wickedness, and every one who can apologize for or excuse it, say they, ought to be blotted from the face of the earth."

6. Elmira, New York, was a notorious Union prison camp known for its high death rate. See James I. Robertson, Jr., "The Scourge of Elmira," in Hesseltine, *Civil War Prisons*, 80–97.

7. Mobile was evacuated on April 11–12. Folmar, *From That Terrible Field*, 158–59. Mosby surrendered at Bettyville, Virginia, on April 17, 1865.

8. Ibid.

9. McPherson, *Ordeal*, 495.

10. This rumor was not correct. General Ewell was captured at Sayler's Creek on April 16 and held at Fort Warren in Boston Harbor. Warner, *Generals*, 85.

11. This rumor was also false. General Edmund Kirby Smith did not surrender his forces until May 26. McPherson, *Ordeal*, 485–86.

12. This was a recurring rumor during the last weeks of the war. On May 19, black troops reportedly attempted to carry out the assassinations of Confederate prisoners in Memphis in retaliation for the Fort Pillow massacre. Hatcher, *The Last Four Weeks*, 334.

13. McPherson, *Ordeal*, 485.

14. Eaton, *Davis*, 260. According to Eaton, "At Greensboro [Davis] summoned Governor [Zebulon] Vance to a conference with his cabinet and General Johnston, . . . the president was bold, defiant, and determined to cross the Mississippi River and continue the fight there."

15. General James Barnes became the commander of Point Lookout Prison in June 1864. A West Point graduate, he was wounded while leading a division at Gettysburg. See Ezra J. Warner, *Generals in Blue: Lives of the Union Commanders* (Baton Rouge: Louisiana State University Press, 1959), 20–21.

16. Williams was released from Point Lookout on June 21, 1865. The camp itself closed at the end of that same month.

# Bibliography

Alabama Department of Archives and History. Civil War Pension Records and Muster Rolls, 40th Alabama Infantry Regiment.

Angle, Paul M., ed. *Three Years in the Army of the Cumberland: The Letters and Diary of Major James A. Connolly.* Bloomington: Indiana University Press, 1959.

Barrett, John G. *Sherman's March Through the Carolinas.* Chapel Hill: University of North Carolina Press, 1956.

Beitzell, Edwin B. *Point Lookout Prison Camp for Confederates.* Privately published, 1972.

Bergeron, Arthur W., Jr. *Guide to Louisiana Confederate Military Units, 1861–1865.* Baton Rouge and London: Louisiana State University Press, 1989.

Black, Robert C. III. *The Railroads of the Confederacy.* Chapel Hill: University of North Carolina Press, 1952.

Bragg, William Harris. *Joe Brown's Army: The Georgia State Line, 1862–1865.* Macon: Mercer University Press, 1987.

Castel, Albert. "Union Fizzle at Atlanta: The Battle of Utoy Church," *Civil War Times Illustrated,* Vol. 16, No. 10 (February 1978): 26–32.

Census of 1860 and 1870. Mobile, Alabama.

Clanahan, James F. *The History of Pickens County, Alabama 1540–1920.* Carrollton, Ala.: Clanahan Publications, n.d.

*Cocoa* [Florida] *Tribune,* 1921.

Connelly, Thomas L. *Autumn of Glory: The Army of Tennessee 1862–1865*. Baton Rouge: Louisiana State University Press, 1971.

Cox, Jacob D. *Atlanta*. New York: Charles Scribner and Sons, 1882.

Cunningham, Horace H. *Doctors in Gray: The Confederate Medical Service*. Baton Rouge: Louisiana State University Press, 1958.

Daniel, Larry J. *Cannoneers in Gray: The Field Artillery of the Army of Tennessee, 1861–1865*. Tuscaloosa and London: University of Alabama Press, 1984.

Davis, Thomas P. Unpublished Civil War Diary, University of South Florida Library Special Collections Department.

Dodson, W. C., ed. *Campaigns of Wheeler and His Cavalry, 1862–1865*. Atlanta: Hudgins Publishing Co., 1899.

Dyer, Frederick H. *A Compendium of the War of the Rebellion*. Three Volumes. New York and London: Thomas Yoseloff, 1959.

Dyer, John P. *From Shiloh to San Juan: The Life of "Fightin' Joe" Wheeler*. Baton Rouge: Louisiana State University Press, 1961.

———. *The Gallant Hood*. Indianapolis and New York: Bobbs-Merrill Co., 1950.

Eaton, Clement. *Jefferson Davis*. New York: Free Press, 1977.

Evans, Clement A., ed. *Confederate Military History*. Volume VII. Atlanta: Confederate Publishing Co., 1899.

Folmar, John Kent, ed. *From That Terrible Field: Civil War Letters of James M. Williams, Twenty-first Alabama Infantry Volunteers*. University, Ala.: University of Alabama Press, 1981.

Foscue, Virginia O. *Place Names in Alabama*. Tuscaloosa and London: University of Alabama Press, 1989.

Griffith, Lucille. *Alabama: A Documentary History to 1900*. University: University of Alabama Press, 1968.

Hardy, John. *Selma: Her Institutions and Her Men*. Spartanburg: Reprint Co., 1978.

Harris, Laurie Lanzen, ed. *Nineteenth-Century Literature Criticism*. Detroit: Gale Research Co., 1981.

Hatcher, Edmund N. *The Last Four Weeks of the War*. Columbus, Ohio: Edmund N. Hatcher, Publisher, 1891.

Hesseltine, William Best. *Civil War Prisons: A Study in War Psychology*. New York: Frederick Ungar Publishing Co., 1964.

Hicken, Victor. *Illinois in the Civil War*. Urbana and London: University of Illinois Press, 1966.

Hood, John B. *Advance and Retreat*. New Orleans: Hood Orphan Memorial Fund, 1880.

Horn, Stanley F. *The Army of Tennessee: A Military History*. Indianapolis and New York: Bobbs-Merrill Co., 1941.

Hughes, Robert M. *General Johnston*. New York: D. Appleton and Co., 1897.

Johnson, Bradley T. *A Memoir of the Life and Public Service of Joseph E. Johnston*. Baltimore: R. H. Woodward, 1891.

Johnston, Joseph E. *Narrative of Military Operations Directed During the Late War Between the States*. Bloomington: Indiana University Press, 1959.

Lash, Jeffrey N. *Destroyer of the Iron Horse: General Joseph E. Johnston and Confederate Rail Transportation, 1861–1865*. Kent: Kent State University Press, 1991.

Lee, Francis Bazley. *Genealogical and Memorial History of the State of New Jersey*. New York: Lewis Historical Publishing Co., 1910.

Lewis, Lloyd. *Sherman: Fighting Prophet*. New York: Harcourt, Brace and Co., 1958.

Linderman, Gerald F. *Embattled Courage: The Experience of Combat in the American Civil War*. New York and London: Free Press, 1987.

Long, E. B. *The Civil War Day By Day: An Almanac 1861–1865*. Garden City: Doubleday, 1971.

McMurry, Richard M. *John Bell Hood and the War for Southern Independence*. Lexington: University Press of Kentucky, 1982.

McPherson, James M. *Ordeal By Fire: The Civil War and Reconstruction*. New York: Alfred A. Knopf, 1982.

Mitchell, Reid. *Civil War Soldiers*. New York: Viking Penquin, 1988.

Mobile [Alabama] *Advertiser and Register*. 1861–1867.

Montgomery [Alabama] *Daily Advertiser*. 1861–1865.

*New York Coachmakers Magazine*. 1860–1862.

Norton, Herman. *Rebel Religion: The Story of Confederate Chaplains*. St. Louis: Bethany Press, 1961.

Owen, Thomas M. *History of Alabama and Dictionary of Alabama Biography*. Volume III. Spartanburg: Reprint Co., 1978.

Pepper, George W. *Personal Recollections of Sherman's Campaigns in Georgia and the Carolinas*. Zanesville, Ohio: Hugh Dunne, 1866.

Ridley, Bromfield L. *Battle Sketches of the Army of Tennessee*. Mexico, Missouri: Missouri Printing and Publishing Co., 1906.

Robertson, James I., Jr. *Soldiers Blue and Gray.* Columbia: University of South Carolina Press, 1988.

Rohrabacher, C. A. *Live Towns and Progressive Men of Florida.* Jacksonville: Times-Union Printing and Publishing House, 1887.

Sherman, William Tecumseh. *Memoirs of General W. T. Sherman.* New York: Literary Classics of the United States, 1990.

*Southern Historical Society Papers.* 52 Volumes. Richmond: Southern Historical Society, 1876–1959.

Sprott, Samuel Henry. "Sumter in the Civil War," *Our Southern Home,* 1899.

Taylor, Robert A. "Rebel Beef: Florida Cattle and the Confederate Army, 1862–1864," *Florida Historical Quarterly* 67 (July 1988), 15–31.

Vicksburg Battlefield National Park. Vicksburg Parole Records.

Warner, Ezra J. *Generals in Blue: Lives of the Union Commanders.* Baton Rouge: Louisiana State University Press, 1959.

———. *Generals in Gray: Lives of Confederate Commanders.* Baton Rouge: Louisiana State University Press, 1959.

*War of the Rebellion: Official Records of the Union and Confederate Armies.* 70 Volumes in 128 parts. Washington, D.C.: Government Printing Office, 1880–1901.

Wiley, Bell I. *The Life of Johnny Reb.* Indianapolis and New York: Bobbs-Merrill Co., 1943.

# Index

Georgia, 13, 28, 35; *place names:*
Adairsville, 72–73; Allatoona,
79–80; Atlanta, 26, 70, 100, 104,
108, 111–12; Augusta, 124; Big
Shanty, 90; Black Creek, 118; Buzzard Roost, 58; Calhoun, 71–72,
117; Camack, 124; Cartersville,
77; Cass County, 73; Cassville,
73–74, 76; Cave Spring, 116;
Cedar Creek, 116; Cedar Point,
115–16; Cobb County, 100; Columbus, 124; Dallas, 115; Dalton,
9, 13, 22–23, 26–27, 34, 63, 71,
99; East Point, 108, 110; Flat
Rock Church, 114; Jonesboro,
110–11; Ken[n]esaw Mountain,
89–91, 115; Lost Mountain, 80,
87–88, 115; McDonough Road,
113; Macon, 124; Macon Road,
108; Marietta, 56, 88, 91, 95;
Mayfield, 124; Milledgeville, 124;
Mill's Gap, 34; Murray County,
36; New Hope Church, 14, 81,
115; Nickajack Creek, 154 (n. 8);
Noyes Creek, 153 (n. 2); Palmetto,
114; Peachtree Creek, 104; Petersburg, 114; Pickett's Mill, 150
(n. 30); Powder Springs Road, 96;
Pumpkin Vine Creek, 150 (n. 32);
Resaca, 22, 56, 64, 69, 71, 117;
Rocky Face, 28, 44, 60, 62; Rome,
116; Sandtown Road, 97; Snake
Creek Gap, 117; Soap Creek, 155
(n. 13); Sparta, 124; Taylor's
Creek, 28, 34, 40, 49; Tilton, 15,
34, 36, 38, 49, 63, 67; Tunnel
Hill, 57; Utoy Church, 108; Van
Wert Mountain, 115; West Point,
105, 108
Gibson, General Randall L., 109
Grant, General Ulysses S., 61, 134

Greenfield [Ohio] *Republican,* 6
Grimley, Lieutenant, 119

Hamilton, Mr. (owner of farm on
Sandtown Road near Atlanta),
98–99
Hamilton, Theodore, 25–26
Hardee, General William J., 111
Hardy, John, 19
Harris, Henry C., 68
Higley, Colonel John H., 9
Hoke, Major General Robert Freder-
ick, 129
Holtzclaw, General James T., 109
Hood, Major General John Bell, 15,
73, 90, 104, 106, 110
"Hudibras," quoted, 32

Illinois, 6; *Union Troop Unit:* 85th
Illinois Regiment, 33
Indiana, 6
Iowa, 6

Johnson, Andrew, 134–35
Johnston, General Joseph Eggleston,
11, 13, 24, 32, 49, 76, 104, 107,
134–36
Jones, Captain William Alexander
Campbell, 27

Kentucky, 83
Kilpatrick, General Judson, 125
Kirby Smith, General Edmund, 83,
135
Know-Nothing Party, 2, 6, 9

Lee, General Robert E., 61, 134–35
Lee, General Stephen D., 110
Lincoln, Abraham, 18, 133–34
Lincoln, Robert, 134
Livingston [Alabama], 7, 121

# About the Editors

**Lewis N. Wynne** is Executive Director, Florida Historical Society. He received his bachelor's, master's, and doctorate from the University of Georgia. He is author of *The Continuity of Cotton: Planter Politics in Georgia, 1865–1892* (1986) and co-editor of *Divided We Fall: Essays on Confederate Nationalism* (1991).

**Robert A. Taylor** is Instructor of History, Indian River Community College. He received his bachelor's and master's from the University of South Florida and his doctorate from Florida State University.